Health, Safety, and Nutrition Activities A to Z

Health, Safety, and Nutrition Activities A to Z

Joanne Matricardi
Jeanne McLarty

THOMSON

DELMAR LEARNING Australia Brazil Canada Mexico Singapore Spain United Kingdom United States

THOMSON

DELMAR LEARNING

Health, Safety, and Nutrition Activities A to Z
Joanne Matricardi and Jeanne McLarty

Vice President, Career Education Strategic Business Unit:
Dawn Gerrain

Director of Learning Solutions:
John Fedor

Managing Editor:
Robert L. Serenka, Jr.

Senior Acquisitions Editor:
Erin O'Connor

Product Manager:
Philip Mandl

Editorial Assistant:
Alison Archambault

Director of Production:
Wendy A. Troeger

Production Manager:
Mark Bernard

Content Project Manager:
Karin Hillen Jaquays

Technology Project Manager:
Sandy Charette

Director of Marketing:
Wendy E. Mapstone

Channel Manager:
Kristin McNary

Marketing Coordinator:
Scott A. Chrysler

Marketing Specialist:
Erica S. Conley

Art Director:
Joy Kocsis

Cover Design:
Joseph Villanova

Any additional questions about permissions can be submitted by email to thomsonrights@thomson.com

Library of Congress Cataloging-in-Publication Data

Matricardi, Joanne.
  Health, safety, and nutrition activities A to Z /
Joanne Matricardi and Jeanne McLarty.
    p. cm.
  Includes bibliographical references and index.
  ISBN-13 978-1-4180-4850-1
  ISBN-10 1-4180-4850-X
  (alk. paper)
  1. Children—Nutrition—Study and teaching (Early childhood)
2. Early childhood education—Activity programs.   3. Children—
Health and hygiene—Study and teaching (Early childhood)
4. Children's accidents—Prevention—Study and teaching
(Early childhood)   I. McLarty, Jeanne.   II. Title.
  TX364.M38 2007
  613.2083—dc22

2007007341

Contents

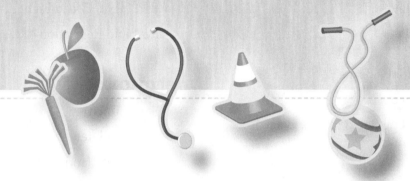

Preface

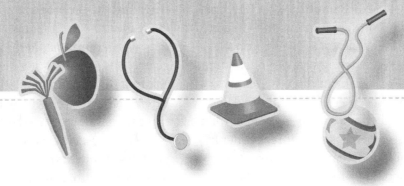

Health, safety, and nutrition are important topics for preschool children. We want to instill in our youth the knowledge and need for a healthy lifestyle. Introducing these topics during the preschool years can assist children in making good choices as they grow older.

The purpose of *Health, Safety, and Nutrition Activities A to Z* is to provide teachers, parents, and student teachers with a collection of activities to promote awareness of these topics. The activities are used across the curriculum, integrating art, blocks, cooking, dramatic play, group time, language arts, manipulatives, math, outdoor play, science, and snack time. Some of them cross curriculum boundaries and may be used in multiple areas.

Health, Safety, and Nutrition Activities A to Z presents activities in an alphabetical layout. This allows adults to link the curriculum to a specific letter of the alphabet. Many classrooms focus on a "letter of the week." This book provides an easy way for health, safety, or nutrition activities to highlight a particular letter.

Some of the lessons offered include the use of patterns in the creation of materials. All suggested patterns are located in the Appendix. The patterns are not meant to use only one time. Materials should be carefully created and preserved for future service. The "Helpful Hints" section of this book contains suggestions for material preservation.

The activities are presented in a lesson plan format. There are five areas: "Developmental Goals," "Learning Objective," "Materials," "Adult Preparation," and "Procedures." The developmental goals offer social-emotional, physical, and cognitive concepts to be explored. The learning objective states what the children will use to accomplish the immediate goal of the lesson. The materials section presents all that is required from the preparation through the implementation of the activity. The procedures section involves a step-by-step process for the child to successfully accomplish the lesson.

Discussion suggestions are given for the activities. These proposals vary between statements to offer the children or possible open-ended questions. Many references are given to the new USDA Food Guide Pyramid. Rather than portions, the new pyramid suggests ounce equivalents. An example of this is in the grain group. A two-year-old child would need 3 ounce equivalents daily. One slice of bread or ½ cup of cooked pasta is an ounce equivalent. When ounce equivalents are discussed, details are provided for the adult. The new Food Guide Pyramid's recommendations are based upon the amount of exercise a person does each day. The suggestions given in this text are based upon individuals receiving less than 30 minutes of physical activity. All information given is available at http://www.mypyramid.gov.

Additional sections may be included in the lesson plan format. At times notes are given for the activity. These notes point out special considerations for the adult. Within the notes section there may be explanations of different outcomes or allergy considerations. Adults need to be aware of the children's health concerns. There have been a growing number of children who have food allergies. Reactions to peanuts or other nuts have become more common. When nuts are used, substitutions are suggested. Milk allergies are also being seen more frequently. Rice or soy milk and vegetable "cheese" products may be exchanged for dairy products. Since most of the recipes are written for an individual child, the substitutions do not need to affect the entire class. Parents are usually very amenable to providing these variations for their child. But once again, be aware of each child's individual needs. Some children are so highly allergic to peanut butter that they may have a reaction without touching it; merely being present in a room where it is being used is enough to cause a reaction.

A growing number of preschool children are vegetarian. Substitutions for these recipes are suggested when meat products are used. The parents of these children are usually very happy to supply the needed soy alternatives.

Some of the nutrition activities make a snack for the child to eat after it's made. In our preschools, we often make a snack and then let the child take it home to share with his or her family. When the food is to be eaten is not always specified in this book. It is up to the discretion of the adult, or check with the policies of the school. Having a child wait to eat what they prepared is a method of practicing delayed gratification. Postponing satisfaction gives the child something to look forward to, offers the opportunity to practice patience, and involves the family.

Safety precautions are also presented when objects used by children may necessitate a need for closer supervision. Book suggestions may be given for an activity. Always review a book before using it with the children. Some of them may not be suitable for all children. If a book appears too long, it is appropriate to paraphrase the text to accommodate shorter attention spans. Expansions for activities are given when another approach may be used to further the lesson.

Age appropriateness for each activity is given. This is just a suggestion. Knowing the children's abilities and attention span will help determine what activities may be done and whether or not they need to be altered.

Health, Safety, and Nutrition Activities A to Z provides several indexes. There are separate indexes for health, safety, and nutrition activities to aid in finding a specific emphasis. The "Curriculum Index" allows the adult to select activities to highlight a particular center. However you choose to implement the use of these activities in your classroom or home is left to your discretion. Whatever you do, have fun! Your enthusiasm will be contagious.

An online resource (http://www. delmarlearning.com/companions/) is an accompaniment to *Health, Safety, and Nutrition Activities A to Z*. This site contains additional group activities for young children. The activities are written in the same lesson plan format found in this book. These detailed plans include developmental goals, learning objectives, a list of materials, directions for adult preparation, and a step-by-step procedure for the child. The activities are easy to understand and implement, either in the preschool classroom or at home. The *Health, Safety, and Nutrition Activities A to Z* online resource also provides links to related preschool sites. These links contain additional ideas, patterns, book sources, and other group time materials.

ACKNOWLEDGMENTS

This book is an accumulation of original and shared ideas developed over 45 years of teaching young children. Many thanks to our co-workers, students, and their parents for sharing and experimenting with us.

We and the editors at Thomson Delmar Learning would also like to thank the following reviewers for their time, effort, and thoughtful contributions which helped to shape the final text:

Lynnette J. McCarty
President, NACCP
Owner, Serendipity Children's Center
Tumwater, Washington

Patricia Capistron
Lead Teacher
Rocking Unicorn Nursery School
West Chatham, Massachusetts

Meredith E. Chambers, M.Ed.
Language Literacy Specialist, Head Teacher
Chinese American Service League-Child
Development Center
Chicago, Illinois

Sandra Hughes
Early Childhood Educator
Rainbow Express Child Care Center
Schenectady, New York

Katherine M. Lozano
Executive Director
Blessed Sacrament Academy Child Development Center
San Antonio, Texas

Vicki Folds, Ed.D.
Curriculum Director, Children of America
Adjunct Professor, Broward Community and
Palm Beach Community College
Parkland, Florida

Marilyn Rice, M.Ed.
Director of Curriculum & Training
Tuckaway Child Development Centers
Mechanicsville, Virginia

Wendy Bertoli
Early Childhood Instructor
Lancaster County Career and Technology
Center
Lancaster, Pennsylvania

Jennifer M. Johnson
Early Childhood Program Head
Vance Granville Community College
Henderson, North Carolina

Christine Pieper, MA
Director of Program Development
Petaluma, California

Joanne Matricardi
Jeanne McLarty

HELPFUL HINTS FOR SUCCESSFUL ACTIVITIES

Throughout the years we've developed strategies that have helped our activities to proceed more smoothly. Some are helpful behavior management tools; others deal with the preservation of materials so that they may be used year after year. The following helpful hints have become routine in our classrooms.

Behavior Management Techniques

✂ The most important aspect of working with young children is that the adults enjoy the activity. Enthusiasm is contagious. Conversely, simply going through the motions of an activity will be noticeable by the children, and their actions will reflect the adult's attitude.

✂ Be prepared. When it is time to start an activity, you should already have all the materials you need. Children will not sit still waiting for you to get ready.

✂ Maintain eye contact with the children. This helps them to sit for longer periods and keeps them interested in the activity.

✂ When reading a book, hold the book open as you read so children can see the pictures. Know the material well enough that you can comfortably glance away from the text. It is important to spend more time looking at the children than looking at the words.

✂ Always keep the group's age and attention span in mind when planning activities. Be flexible. A group activity may need to be cut short if the attention is waning.

✄ Alternate quiet and active activities. Too many quiet plans may cause the children to lose interest. Too many active ones many cause them to become overstimulated.

Preservation of Materials

✄ When creating materials, use rubber cement for gluing; white glue may cause paper to wrinkle.

✄ If possible, laminate all materials made with paper. A laminator may be purchased for $350 to $1500. Some school supply or office supply stores will laminate materials for a set fee.

✄ If you do not have access to a laminator, use clear, unpatterned contact paper or heavy tag board.

✄ Store materials in resealable plastic bags. This allows you to see at a glance what is inside and makes storage in a filing cabinet or file box easier.

Miscellaneous

✄ Making song posters encourages all adults in the room to sing along. Adult involvement is important to encourage all the children to participate. Adults don't need to feel self-conscious regarding the quality of their singing. Children are nonjudgmental and enjoy singing as a joyful experience.

✄ Song posters are also beneficial to the preschooler. Although these children cannot read, using a poster with the song written on it provides a pre-reading enrichment as it calls attention to the printed word. The use of illustrations on the poster can also help the children to identify the song.

✄ Some activities will work great for one group of children and not for others. This may vary from year to year. If an activity fails, do not assume it is totally the adult's responsibility. The make-up of the group may play a large role in the success of an activity. At times, an activity may work better later in the year, when the children have matured. Always take time for reflection and self-evaluation.

Ask yourself, "What made the activity a success?" or "Is there something that can be improved upon?"

SAFETY PRECAUTIONS

Some of the nutrition activities involve cooking. These activities may require additional safety precautions. The following practices are standard in our classrooms.

✄ Wash all fruits and vegetables thoroughly with running water. *Vegetarian Times* cautions against using soap, since the produce will absorb it (Hise, 2004).

✄ Check the center's policies. Some schools will not allow the use of heating elements in the classroom and require the adults to heat or bake food in the kitchen.

✄ When using a hot plate or electric skillet, roll towels and place them around the appliance to create a buffer between the heat and the child.

✄ If the adult needs to leave the room, lift the electric appliance out of reach. Make sure the cord is also out of reach.

✄ Do not leave cords plugged into an outlet once the appliance has been detached. This is like leaving an outlet uncovered.

✄ If using equipment with cords, tape the cord to the table and floor. This is to ensure the appliance doesn't get pulled off the table by a dangling cord, and also prevents people from tripping over cords on the floor.

✄ Always supervise children closely when cooking. Small foods may present a choking hazard in young children.

SUPPLIES NEEDED

Most early childhood programs operate on a limited budget. Many of the materials we use in this book may be purchased at your local dollar store. The shopping list that follows has been divided into six categories: consumables, non-consumables, equipment, kitchen equipment, food, and recyclable items.

CONSUMABLE SUPPLIES

Adhesive bandages
Adhesive labels
Alcohol pads
Aluminum foil
Blank video tape
Brads
Candle
Card stock paper
Clear contact paper
Colored pencils
Confetti
Construction paper
Copy paper
Cotton balls
Cotton swabs
Crayons
Dental floss
Dish soap
Florescent paint
Foam balls
Foam bowls
Foam plates
Gauze
Glue
Glue sticks
Hook and loop tape
Hot glue sticks
Ice pack (empty)
Index cards
Jumbo foil muffin
   liners
Markers (permanent)
Markers (water base)
Masking tape
Paper bags (lunch-size)
Paper plates
Paper towels
Pencils
Pipe cleaners
Plastic forks
Plastic spoons
Poster board
Rubber cement
Rubbing alcohol
Staples
Stickers (assorted)
Tempera paint
Tissue
Tongue depressors
Yarn
Zinc oxide

NONCONSUMABLE SUPPLIES

Adult-size belts
   with buckle
Baby bottles
Baskets
Bath towels
Beads
Blankets
Blindfold
Blood pressure cuff
Bottle (small)
Cash register
Coin purse
Combs (large-tooth)
Dishcloth
Dishpan
Dolls
Flashlight
Glass jar
Glasses without lenses
Hair dryer (cord
   removed)
Headbands
Helmets (assorted)
Hole puncher
Lighter
Long scarves
Melon scooper
Paddle (ping pong or
   paddle ball)
Pictures of helmets
Play money
Pool (small wading
   pool)
Road map
Rhythm sticks
Scissors (adult)
Scissors (child)
Small toy people
Smocks
Snap clothespins
Stapler
Stethoscope
Stretch bandage roll
String
Stuffed dogs
Tablecloth
Telephone
Timer
Toy blood pressure cuff
Toy dishes
Toy food

Utility knife
Wallet
Watch with second hand
Whistle
X-rays
Yardstick

EQUIPMENT

Black light
Camera
CD player
Child-size chairs
Child-size rocker
Doll beds
Hot glue gun
Plastic tarp
Tape recorder
Toy cars
Toy trucks
Video camera
Wooden blocks
Wooden planks

KITCHEN EQUIPMENT

Apple slicer/corer
Baking sheet
Bowls (assorted sizes)
Colander
Crock pot
Cups (small)
Cups and saucers
Cutting board
Electric skillet
Grater
Knife
Ladle
Large pot
Long handled wooden
   spoon
Measuring cups
Measuring spoons
Paring knife
Pitcher (adult-size)
Pitcher (child-size)
Plastic bowls
Potato masher
Rolling pin
   (adult-size)
Rolling pin (child-size)
Smooth edge can
   opener
Spoons

Table knives
Tea kettle
Tongs
Vegetable peeler

FOOD

15 oz. can carrots
   (sliced)
15 oz. can corn
15 oz. can cut green
   beans
15 oz. can kidney
   beans
15 oz. can sliced
   potato
15 oz. can vegetable
   broth
Apple
Apricot
Artichoke
Baking powder
Bananas
Bread (wheat)
Butter or margarine
Cantaloupe
Carrots (fresh)
Cheese (shredded
   and sliced)
Cinnamon
Decaffeinated coffee
Decaffeinated greet tea
   (assorted flavors)
Deli chicken sliced
   meat
Deli ham sliced meat
Deli turkey sliced meat
Eggs
Egg substitute
Elbow macaroni
French bread (long)
Frozen bread dough
Granola
Ground beef
Honey
Honeydew melon
Leeks
Lemon Juice
Lettuce
Mayonnaise
Mustard
Oatmeal (quick
   cooking)
Olive oil

Onion (yellow, medium)
Peanut butter
Pepper
Potatoes
Raisins (black)
Raisins (golden)
Rice
Salt
Salty potato chips
Self-rising flour

Sour pickles
Spaghetti sauce
Sugar
Tomatoes
Tomato sauce
Vegetable oil
Watermelon
Whole wheat flour
Yogurt (assorted flavors)
Zucchini

RECYCLABLE ITEMS
Appliance box
Conditioner bottle
  (empty)
Food labels
Magazines
Newspapers
Paper bags (grocery)
Paper towel tubes

Peroxide bottle
  (empty)
Prescription bottles
  (empty)
Shampoo bottle (empty)
Sunscreen bottles
  (empty)
Vitamin bottles
  (empty)

Air Quality

AGES: 3–5

GROUP SIZE:
2–3 children

DEVELOPMENTAL GOALS:

✂ To stimulate observation skills

✂ To encourage environmental awareness

LEARNING OBJECTIVE:

Using a jar, string, liquid watercolor, and water, the child will simulate pollution.

MATERIALS:

Scissors
String
Small bottle
Ice cubes
Cold water
Pitcher (child-size)
Measuring cup
Large clear jar
Black liquid watercolor

ADULT PREPARATION:

1. Cut a length of string approximately 12".
2. Tie both ends around the neck of the small bottle to make a loop for a handle.
3. Put ice cubes and water in a child-size pitcher.
4. Microwave 1 cup of water for 1–2 minutes.

PROCEDURES:

The child will complete the following steps:

1. Pour cold water into the large jar filling it 2/3 full.
2. Add black watercolor to the small bottle.

The adult will complete the following steps:

1. Pour hot water into the small bottle.
2. Lower the small bottle into the large jar of cold water.
3. Ask the child, "What is happening?"

continued

Air Quality continued

NOTE:

The hot water will rise up to the top of the large jar, simulating pollution in the air.

DISCUSSION SUGGESTIONS:

- ✂ Dirty air from cars, factories, etc.
- ✂ Dirty air is difficult to breathe.
- ✂ Some days you can see the dirt in the air. This is called smog.
- ✂ Some places are trying to improve the air quality by checking the *emissions* a car makes, and making them get repaired if the air quality from the car is dirty. Many factories are also trying to clean up the *emissions* they put in the air.

BOOK SUGGESTIONS:

- ✂ *The Lorax* by Dr. Seuss. (New York: Random House, 1971). Dr. Seuss tells the tale of a creature that pollutes a beautiful land.
- ✂ Bill Peet's *Wump World* (Boston: Houghton-Mifflin, 1970). The Wump's planet is destroyed by the Pollutians.

Apples, Apricots, and Artichokes

ADULT PREPARATION:

1. Purchase or ask parents to send in an apple, apricot, and artichoke.
2. Copy, color, and cut out multiple patterns of the apple, apricot, and artichoke patterns (make at least four of each item).
3. Cut the construction paper into squares and glue the individual food copies on each square.
4. Place the three foods on the table.
5. Place the food cards in a stack, face down, on the table.

PROCEDURES:

The child will complete the following steps:

1. Touch and name each of the three foods.
2. Place the three foods in a line from left to right.
3. Pick a card from the top of the stack.
4. Name the food and set the card in front of the matching apple, apricot, or artichoke.
5. Continue until all cards have been turned over and matched.

NOTE:

Start with two of each card for two-year-olds, and increase the number of cards as the child's skill increases.

DISCUSSION SUGGESTIONS:

- ✄ Apples and apricots are part of the fruit group. Children between the ages of 2 and 8 need 1–1½ cups of fruit daily.
- ✄ Artichokes are part of the vegetable group. Children between the ages of 2 and 8 need 1–1½ cups of vegetables daily.
- ✄ Serving sizes differ depending upon the age and activity level of each person. Check www.mypyramid.gov for more details.

BOOK SUGGESTION:

Arthur's Artichoke by Geoffrey Moss (New York: Dial Press, 1970). Arthur turns an artichoke into a pet.

AGES: 2½–5

GROUP SIZE:
2–5 children

DEVELOPMENTAL GOALS:
- ✄ To develop language skills
- ✄ To promote visual discrimination

LEARNING OBJECTIVE:
Using an apple, apricot, artichoke, and pictures of the foods, the child will identify and match pictures to food.

MATERIALS:
Apple
Apricot
Artichoke
Copy paper
Patterns of an apple, apricot, and artichoke (Appendix A1)
Scissors
Construction paper
Markers, colored pencils, or crayons
Rubber cement

AGES: 3–5

GROUP SIZE:
4–16 children

DEVELOPMENTAL GOALS:
✂ To promote safety
✂ To increase vocabulary

LEARNING OBJECTIVE:
Using pictures of potential accidents, the child will tell how to avoid accidents in the home.

MATERIALS:
Avoiding accident card patterns (Appendix A2–A7):
Stairs with safety gate open (Appendix A2)
Electrical outlet with covers beside it on floor (Appendix A3)
Electrical cord draped across the floor (Appendix A4)
Hot stove (Appendix A5)
Cabinet door open showing cleaning items (Appendix A6)
Hot water in bathtub (Appendix A7)
Copy paper
Markers, colored pencils, or crayons
Scissors
Rubber cement
Construction paper

Avoiding Accidents

ADULT PREPARATION:
1. Make and color a copy of each avoiding accident card pattern.
2. Cut and glue the pattern on a square of construction paper.

PROCEDURES:
The children will complete the following steps:
1. Look at one of the avoiding accident cards.
2. Explain what is unsafe about the picture.
3. Explain what can be done to make the situation safe.

DISCUSSION SUGGESTIONS:
✂ Ask the child what is unsafe in each picture.
✂ Ask the child what might happen to a person if the unsafe situation is not changed.
✂ Ask the child what can be done to change the situation to a safe one.
✂ Assist the child with answers if none are known.

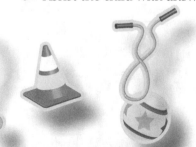

Backseat Baby

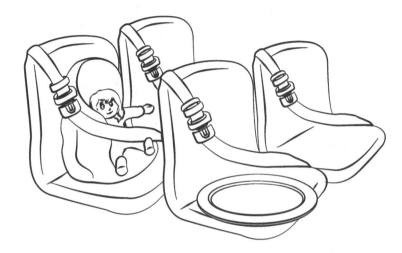

AGES: 4–5

GROUP SIZE:
4–6 children

DEVELOPMENTAL GOALS:
- ✂ To encourage social development
- ✂ To increase fine motor skills

LEARNING OBJECTIVE:
Using a car seat, baby doll, chairs, and a plate, the children will use fine motor skills to buckle a baby into a seat.

MATERIALS:
Four chairs
Plate
Car seat
Four adult-size belts with buckles
Baby doll

ADULT PREPARATION:

1. Place chairs to resemble a car.
2. Put a plate on the driver's seat to use as a steering wheel.
3. Put the car seat on one of the back chairs. Fix the car seat to the chair with a belt so it doesn't move.
4. Loop the remaining belts around the other chairs to use as seat belts.

PROCEDURES:

The children complete the following steps:

1. Listen to the adult explain that a car seat must be in the back seat for the baby to be safe.
2. Watch the adult demonstrate how to buckle and unbuckle the car seat.
3. Assign roles: driver, front seat passenger, and baby's caregiver.
4. The driver and front seat passenger take their seats and buckle their "seat belts."
5. The baby's care giver straps the doll into the car seat, then sits beside the baby and buckles his or her "seat belt."
6. The driver may pretend to take the passengers to a specific destination.
7. The children may take turns at different roles and repeat steps 3–6.

continued

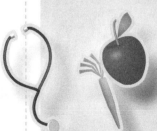

Backseat Baby continued

DISCUSSION SUGGESTIONS:

- ✂ Check the state laws for age requirements.
- ✂ All children under a specific age must be strapped into a car seat.
- ✂ All people not in a car seat must wear a seat belt.
- ✂ It is always safer for a child to sit in the back seat.
- ✂ Children under the age of 12 may not sit in the front seat when there are air bags.
- ✂ Air bags are to keep adult-sized people safe.

Banana

AGES: 2½–5

GROUP SIZE:
3–6 children

DEVELOPMENTAL GOALS:
- ✂ To practice cooking procedures
- ✂ To develop fine motor skills

LEARNING OBJECTIVE:
Using banana, granola, honey, a plate, bowl, plastic knife, spoon, and a tablespoon, the child will make a nutritious snack.

MATERIALS:
Banana
Cutting board
Bowls
Granola
Honey
Plate
Plastic knife
Spoon
Tablespoon

ADULT PREPARATION:

1. Wash hands.
2. Place banana on the cutting board.
3. Cut banana in half and put it in a large bowl.
4. Place granola and honey in separate bowls.

PROCEDURES:

The child will complete the following steps:
1. Wash hands.
2. Select a banana half and peel it. Discard the peel.
3. Slice the banana on a plate using the plastic knife.
4. Place the banana slices in a bowl.
5. Drizzle honey on the bananas with a spoon.
6. Add 2 tablespoons of granola over the banana.

continued

Banana continued

DISCUSSION SUGGESTIONS:

- ✂ Bananas are a wonderful fruit.
- ✂ They are full of vitamins and minerals.
- ✂ They provide energy and help ease stress.
- ✂ Bananas do not have to require any preparation. Just peel and eat!

BOOK SUGGESTIONS:

- ✂ *I Want My Banana!* by Mary Risk (New York: Barron's Educational Series, Inc., 1996). Monkey looks for his lost banana in this book. This book is written in both English and Spanish.
- ✂ For a factual book on bananas for five-year-olds, read *Bananas* by Elaine Landau (New York: Children's Press, 1999).

Blindness

ADULT PREPARATION:

1. Clear an area where the children can safely walk.

PROCEDURES:

The child will complete the following steps:

1. Listen to the adult explain, "Some people cannot see with their eyes, like we do. They have people, dogs, or canes that help them move around."
2. Be paired with a partner.
3. Select roles: one is the blind (visually impaired) person, the other is the assistant.
4. The visually impaired person puts on the blindfold.
5. The assistant guides the first child around the room, to a chair, to a closet, or cubby, etc.
6. The children may reverse roles and repeat steps 4–5.

DISCUSSION SUGGESTIONS:

✂ When you guide a blind person, let him hold your arm a little higher than the elbow.

✂ When you guide a blind person, tell him where you are leading him.

✂ Tell the blind person when you approach stairs and if you are going to go up or down.

✂ For more information visit http://www.abwa.asn.au/body_sightedguide.html, for an article on guiding a blind person from the Web site of The Association for the Blind of Western Australia.

AGES: 3–5

GROUP SIZE:

4–6 children

DEVELOPMENTAL GOALS:

✂ To develop an awareness of the sense of sight

✂ To promote social development

LEARNING OBJECTIVE:

Using a blindfold and a partner, the child will walk with assistance.

MATERIALS:

Blindfold

Blood Pressure

AGES: 3–5

GROUP SIZE:

2 children

DEVELOPMENTAL GOALS:

✂ To enhance listening skills

✂ To encourage sharing

LEARNING OBJECTIVE:

Using a toy blood pressure cuff and stethoscope, the child will take blood pressure.

MATERIALS:

Blood pressure cuff
Stethoscope
Toy blood pressure cuff
Alcohol pads or rubbing alcohol and cotton balls

ADULT PREPARATION:

1. Set blood pressure cuff, stethoscope, and the toy blood pressure cuff on the table.
2. Wipe ear pieces of the stethoscope with an alcohol wipe, or use a cotton ball with alcohol.
3. Keep alcohol pads or rubbing alcohol and cotton balls out of the reach of children.

PROCEDURES:

The child will complete the following:

1. Watch as the adult uses the real blood pressure cuff by putting it on a child's arm.
2. Put the stethoscope on the bend of the child's arm above the blood pressure cuff to hear the heartbeat.
3. Put the stethoscope in the ears to hear his or her heartbeat.
4. Listen to the adult say, "This is what doctors and nurses use to check your blood pressure."
5. Use a toy stethoscope to take another child's blood pressure.

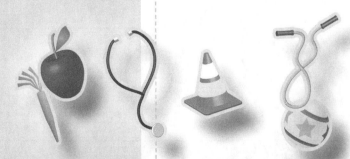

continued

Blood Pressure continued

6. Listen to his or her heartbeat with the stethoscope.

7. Watch the teacher wipe the ear pieces of the stethoscope with an alcohol wipe.

8. Children take turns taking each other's blood pressure with the toy blood pressure cuff and stethoscope.

NOTE:

This activity may start in group time and then move to the dramatic play center.

DISCUSSION SUGGESTIONS:

✂ Blood pressure changes during the day.

✂ Blood pressure is the lowest when a person is sleeping.

✂ Blood pressure can go higher when a person is nervous, excited, or active.

Class Cookbook

AGES: 2½–5

GROUP SIZE:

2–5 children

DEVELOPMENTAL GOALS:

✄ To involve families

✄ To participate in a group activity

LEARNING OBJECTIVE:

Using construction paper, markers, brads, a hole puncher, and adhesive labels, the child will make his or her own class cookbook.

MATERIALS:

Family Letter 1
    (Appendix B1)
Recipe form
    (Appendix B2)
Copy paper
Hole punch
Construction paper
Permanent markers
Adhesive labels
Brads

ADULT PREPARATION:

1. Copy and send home the family letter and recipe form with each child.
2. Make copies of each recipe equal to the number of children in the group.
3. Punch three holes on the side of the recipes.
4. Punch corresponding holes on two pieces of construction paper for each child. The construction paper will be the front and back cover.
5. Using a permanent marker, write *My Class Cookbook* on an adhesive label for each child.

PROCEDURES:

The child will complete the following steps:

1. Color the cover with markers.
2. Peel the adhesive label with *My Class Cookbook* and stick it to the front cover.

The adult will complete the following step:

1. Assemble the book using brads to secure the pages.

continued

Class Cookbook continued

NOTE:

Older children may help with the construction of the recipe book as outlined in the adult procedures.

DISCUSSION SUGGESTIONS:

- ✂ What is the child's favorite food?
- ✂ What are the types of food groups used in the recipe?

Cover Your Cough

AGES: 3–5

GROUP SIZE:

4–6 children

DEVELOPMENTAL GOALS:

- ✂ To stimulate healthy habits
- ✂ To develop fine motor skills

LEARNING OBJECTIVE:

Using a tissue, face cutout, construction paper, pencil, crayons, scissors, and glue, the child will create a picture of a healthy habit.

MATERIALS:

Confetti
Bowl
Copy paper
Face pattern
    (Appendix A8)
Adult scissors
Spoon
Balloon
Glue
Pencil
Child safety scissors
Construction paper
Crayons

ADULT PREPARATION:

1. Put confetti in bowl.
2. Make a copy of the face pattern. Cut out one pattern per child.

PROCEDURES:

The child will complete the following steps:

1. Listen to adult explain, "If we cough or sneeze without covering our mouth, germs go through the air and spread. Germs cannot be seen."
2. Watch adult place three spoonfuls of confetti inside flat balloon and then blow balloon halfway up and squeeze the top closed.
3. Watch adult hold balloon beside mouth and pretend to sneeze when he or she stops squeezing the top of the balloon. The confetti will spray out like germs spreading in the air.
4. Sit at a table with the cutout of the face, tissue, glue, pencil, scissors, construction paper, and crayons.
5. Trace hand with pencil on construction paper, using adult assistance if necessary.
6. Cut out traced hand, with adult assistance if needed.
7. Draw in eyes, mouth, and nose with crayons.
8. Glue tissue over mouth.
9. Place a small amount of glue on the traced hand.
10. Place the cut out of traced hand on the tissue.

NOTE:

Older child may cut out face pattern.

DISCUSSION SUGGESTIONS:

- ✂ To keep people healthy, we need to cover our mouth with a tissue when we cough or sneeze to prevent the spread of germs.
- ✂ The project is a reminder to always cover your cough or sneeze.

Crossing the Street

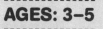

AGES: 3–5

GROUP SIZE:

2–4 children

DEVELOPMENTAL GOALS:

✀ To develop problem-solving ability

✀ To coordinate large and small muscles

LEARNING OBJECTIVE:

Using blocks, road mat, cars, and small toy people, the child will practice looking both ways before crossing the street.

MATERIALS:

Road mat
Blocks
Cars
Small toy people

ADULT PREPARATION:

1. Place road mat on the floor in the block area.

PROCEDURES:

The child will complete the following steps:

1. Build road with blocks.
2. Place cars on road.
3. Put small toy people near road.
4. Listen to the teacher say, "The people need to cross the road. What should they do to be safe?"
5. Have small toy people look both ways before crossing the street.
6. If small toy people have movable arms, have them hold hands while crossing, as children need to hold an adult's hand before crossing the street.

DISCUSSION SUGGESTIONS:

✀ Why is it important to look both ways before crossing the street?
✀ Why should a child hold an adult's hand when crossing the street?

Dental Bags

AGES: 2½–5

GROUP SIZE:

6–12 children

DEVELOPMENTAL GOALS:

- ✄ To increase vocabulary
- ✄ To become familiar with dental hygiene

LEARNING OBJECTIVE:

Using dental welcome bags and a tooth-brushing chart, the child will practice dental hygiene.

MATERIALS:

Dental welcome bags from local dentist (including toothpaste, dental floss, and toothbrush)
Copy paper
Family Letter 2 (Appendix B3)
Tooth-brushing chart (Appendix B4)

ADULT PREPARATION:

1. Ask a dentist for dental welcome bags.
2. If the following items are not in the bag, purchase one for each child:
   a. Toothpaste
   b. Dental floss
   c. Toothbrush
3. Copy the tooth-brushing chart for each child.
4. Copy and complete the family letter.
5. Attach the chart to the family letter to send home.
6. Clear an area for group time.

PROCEDURES:

The children will complete the following steps:

1. Take turns pulling an item out of the dental welcome bag.
2. Identify the item and tell how it is used.
3. Replace the item in the bag.
4. Take the bag home with the family letter and tooth-brushing chart.
5. Fill out the chart at home.

DISCUSSION SUGGESTIONS:

- ✄ How many times should we brush and floss our teeth?
- ✄ When should we brush and floss our teeth?
- ✄ Why should we brush and floss our teeth?

BOOK SUGGESTIONS:

- ✄ *Does a Tiger Open Wide?* by Red Ehrlich (New York: Blue Apple Books, 2003). This book, accompanied by colorful illustrations, examines who goes to the dentist and what is done there.
- ✄ The reader is shown a young girl's first visit to the dentist through large photographs on each page in *First Visit to the Dentist* by Monica Hughes (Chicago: Raintree, 2004).

16

Diet Detectives

food chart

AGES: 3–5

GROUP SIZE:
6–12 children

DEVELOPMENTAL GOALS:
- ✂ To promote parent involvement with nutrition
- ✂ To enhance counting skills

LEARNING OBJECTIVE:
Using a food chart, the children will count food items and create a graph.

MATERIALS:
Family Letter 3 (Appendix B5)
Food chart (Appendix B6)
Copy paper
Poster board
Yardstick
Markers (orange, green, red, blue, and purple)

ADULT PREPARATION:

1. Copy the family letter and food chart for each child.
2. Make a graph out of poster board using a yardstick and markers.
3. Divide the poster board into five columns.
4. Divide the columns with horizontal lines equally, two squares for each column per child in the class.
5. At the bottom of each column write one of the five healthy food groups. Use the colors of the Food Guide Pyramid:

   a. Grains (orange marker)

   b. Vegetables (green marker)

   c. Fruits (red marker)

   d. Milk and dairy products (blue marker)

   e. Meat, beans, fish, and nuts (purple marker)

continued

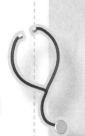

Diet Detectives continued

PROCEDURES:

The children will complete the following steps:

1. Take the family letter and food chart home.
2. Fill in the food chart with the foods eaten for dinner.
3. Return the chart to school.
4. Take turns saying what they ate for dinner (the adult will prompt them by looking at their chart if they forgot a food).
5. Watch the adult write the type of food eaten in the appropriate column.
6. Once all children's foods are on the chart, repeat after adult the food in each column (i.e., The grains group has the following foods—rice, "rice"; spaghetti, "spaghetti"; biscuit, "biscuit"; bread, "bread").
7. Count the number of food types in each column.

DISCUSSION SUGGESTIONS:

✀ People need to eat food from all the food groups to stay healthy.

✀ Eating foods from all the groups helps you get all the vitamins and nutrients you need.

✀ If a child didn't eat from one of the groups, ask what type of food they like from that group. Give suggestions if the child cannot answer.

Dogs Can Be Strangers Too

DOGS CAN BE STRANGER TOO

AGES: 2–5

GROUP SIZE:
4–12 children

DEVELOPMENTAL GOALS:
- ✂ To develop vocabulary
- ✂ To promote social development

LEARNING OBJECTIVE:
Using a song board and stuffed toy dogs, the children will participate in a song.

MATERIALS:
Markers
Poster board
Stuffed toy dogs

ADULT PREPARATION:

1. Using markers, write the words to *Dogs Can Be Strangers Too* on the poster board.
2. Arrange a stuffed toy dog at each child's place for group time.

PROCEDURES:

The children will complete the following step:

1. Stand with the stuffed toy dog in front of them and sing the following song to the tune of *Mary Had a Little Lamb*:

Dogs Can be Strangers Too

I met a stranger dog named Boo   *(Child keeps arms and hands to their side.)*

continued

Dogs Can Be Strangers Too continued

His name was Boo,
His name was Boo,
I met a stranger dog named Boo,
His owner was there too.

I asked his owner if he'd play,
If he'd play,
If he'd play,
I asked his owner if he'd play,
Then I showed him my hand

(Child lets stuffed toy dog smell the BACK of their hand.)

I met a stranger dog named Bear

(Child keeps arms and hands to their side.)

Her name was Bear,
Her name was Bear,
I met a stranger dog named Bear,
Her owner was not there.

I slowly backed away from her

(Child backs away from stuffed toy dog.)

Away from her,
Away from her,
I slowly backed away from her,
I went off to play.

DISCUSSION SUGGESTIONS:

- ✄ Why is it unsafe to go up to a dog you do not know?
- ✄ Always ask the owner if you can pet the dog and how the dog likes to be petted.

Exit Hunt

AGES: $2\frac{1}{2}$–5

GROUP SIZE:

6–12 children

DEVELOPMENTAL GOALS:

- ✂ To expand vocabulary
- ✂ To enhance listening skills

LEARNING OBJECTIVE:

Using a copy of the exit sign, children will go on an exit hunt.

MATERIALS:

Exit sign pattern (Appendix A9)
Copy paper
Red marker or crayon

ADULT PREPARATION:

1. Make a copy of the exit sign pattern.
2. Color the border and letters red.

PROCEDURES:

The children will complete the following steps:

1. Sit on the floor in a semicircle or circle.
2. Pass around the exit sign.
3. Listen to the adult explain, "You should always know where the exits are located. They are signs above doors that light up in the dark; these signs show us how to get out of the building."
4. Walk around the building looking for exit signs.
5. Count the number of exit signs found.

DISCUSSION SUGGESTIONS:

- ✂ When do you go through an exit?
- ✂ What makes a door an emergency exit?

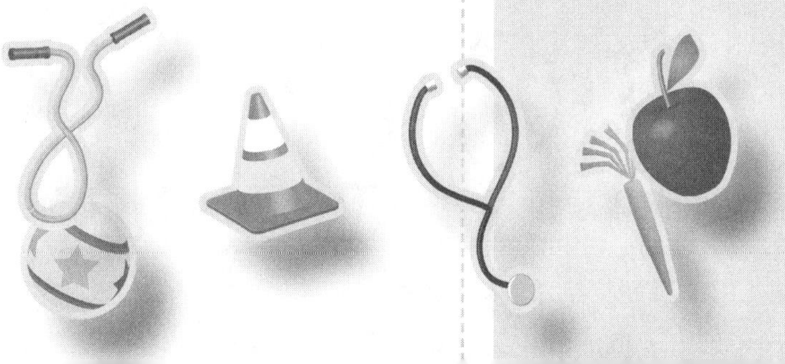

Exercise Video

GROUP SIZE:

6–16 children

DEVELOPMENTAL GOALS:

- ✂ To develop large muscles
- ✂ To practice balance and coordination

LEARNING OBJECTIVE:

Using a CD and CD player, the children will exercise while being videotaped.

MATERIALS:

Permission form to be photographed and videotaped (Appendix B7)
Video camera
Blank video tape
CD player
CD featuring large muscle activities, such as the *Hokey Pokey*

ADULT PREPARATION:

1. Ask a parent volunteer or a staff member to help videotape.
2. Make sure each child has a permission form to be videotaped on file.

PROCEDURES:

The children will complete the following steps:

1. Line up in rows, facing the camera.
2. Follow the directions on the CD.
3. Once the first song is finished, have the front row move to the back, and the other rows move forward.
4. Follow the directions on a second song.
5. After each song, have the first row move to the back, and the other rows move forward.

SONG SUGGESTIONS:

- ✂ *The Hokey Pokey,* Executive Producer: Stephen Fite (1992). (Melody House, 819 N.W. 92nd St., Okalahoma City, OK 72114)
- ✂ "Listen and Move" on the CD, *We all Live Together,* Volume 2, by Greg & Steve (Youngheart Records, P.O. 6017, Cypress, CA 90630).

DISCUSSION SUGGESTIONS:

- ✂ Why is exercise good for you?
- ✂ Is it easier to exercise in a group or alone?
- ✂ What is your favorite exercise or sport?

Extreme Eggs

AGES: 2½–5

GROUP SIZE:
2–6 children

DEVELOPMENTAL GOALS:
✂ To develop self-help skills

✂ To stimulate fine motor control

LEARNING OBJECTIVE:
Using an egg, shredded cheese, muffin liner, fork, bowl, and tablespoon, the child will make an individual portion of eggs.

MATERIALS:
Shredded cheese
Bowl
Foil muffin liners
Permanent marker
Eggs (one for each child)
Fork
Tablespoon
Baking sheet

ADULT PREPARATION:

1. Preheat oven to 350°.
2. Wash hands.
3. Place shredded cheese in a bowl.
4. Write child's name on the bottom of muffin liner with a permanent marker.
5. Remove the paper insert from the muffin liner.
6. Crack the egg and put it in a bowl. Discard the shells.

continued

23

Extreme Eggs continued

PROCEDURES:

The child will complete the following steps:

1. Wash hands.
2. Select a bowl with an egg.
3. Use a fork to beat the egg.
4. Add 2 tablespoons of shredded cheese and mix well.
5. Select the muffin liner with his or her name written on the bottom.

The adult will complete the following steps:

1. Assist the child in pouring the egg mixture into the foil muffin liner.
2. Place the muffin liner on the baking sheet.
3. Once the baking sheet is full, bake for approximately 20 minutes or until the eggs are firm.

DISCUSSION SUGGESTIONS:

✃ Eggs are a good source of protein.
✃ Complete protein is needed for the body to build its own protein.

NOTE:

If using large or jumbo eggs, jumbo muffin liners may be needed.

 ### SAFETY PRECAUTION:

Always wash hands after handling eggs.

Finger Prints

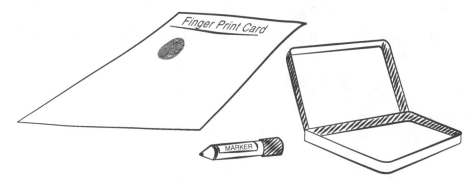

Finger Print Card

MARKER

AGES: 2½–5

GROUP SIZE:
1 child per adult

DEVELOPMENTAL GOALS:
- ✂ To develop eye-hand coordination
- ✂ To recognize their name

LEARNING OBJECTIVE:
Using a fingerprint card and washable stamp pad, the child will make their fingerprints.

MATERIALS:
Fingerprint card pattern (Appendix B8)
Card stock paper
Permanent marker
Washable stamp pad

ADULT PREPARATION:

1. Make a copy of the fingerprint card for each child on card stock paper.
2. Write each child's full name in the appropriate section of the card.

PROCEDURES:

The child will complete the following steps:

1. Select the fingerprint card with his or her name.
2. Press right thumb on stamp pad.
3. With adult assistance, roll their thumb from left to right on the right thumb section of the fingerprint card.
4. Repeat steps 2–3 with each finger of the right hand.
5. Repeat steps 2–3 with each finger of the left hand.
6. Wash hands.

NOTE:

The teacher, parents, or guardians may fill out the remainder of the information at the top of the card.

DISCUSSION SUGGESTIONS:

- ✂ An identification card for children is like a parent's driver's license.
- ✂ It helps provide information in an emergency.

First Aid

AGES: 3–5

GROUP SIZE:

2–4 children

DEVELOPMENTAL GOALS:

- ✂ To develop language skills
- ✂ To role-play a life situation

LEARNING OBJECTIVE:

Using a doll, adhesive bandage, gauze, empty ice pack, cotton balls, stretch bandage roll, and an empty bottle of hydrogen peroxide, the child will role-play giving first aid.

MATERIALS:

Empty bottle of
  hydrogen peroxide
Doll
Adhesive bandage
Gauze
Ice pack (empty)
Cotton balls
Stretch bandage roll

ADULT PREPARATION:

1. Wash bottle of hydrogen peroxide to ensure no chemical is left in the bottle.
2. Clear area for group time.

PROCEDURES:

The child completes the following steps:

1. Sit in a circle or semicircle.
2. Listen to adult explain, "When someone gets hurt, you help them by cleaning their scrape and putting on adhesive bandages or a bandage. When you do this you are giving first aid."
3. Identify the following items as they are passed around the circle: adhesive bandage, gauze, ice pack (empty), cotton balls, stretch bandage roll, hydrogen peroxide bottle (empty).
4. Watch as the adult demonstrates how to use each item on the doll.
5. Move all items to the dramatic play area.
6. Take turns using the first aid items on the doll.

DISCUSSION SUGGESTIONS:

- ✂ First aid is important so people will know how to treat others who are hurt.
- ✂ Knowing first aid also helps you know when to call for help.

Floss Your Teeth

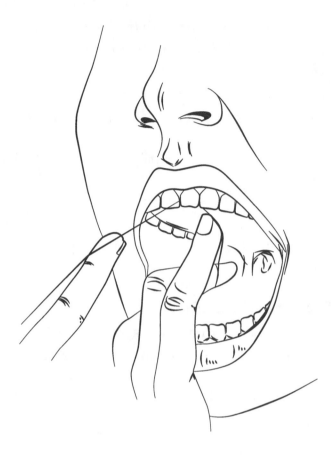

AGES: 2–5

GROUP SIZE:
2–5 children

DEVELOPMENTAL GOALS:
- ✂ To promote dental hygiene
- ✂ To enhance fine motor skills

LEARNING OBJECTIVE:
Using a brown tooth cut-out, white tempera paint, dental floss, and smock, the child will whiten a tooth.

MATERIALS:
Tooth pattern (Appendix A10)
Copy paper
Marker
Brown construction paper
Scissors
White tempera paint
Foam plate
Dish soap
Spoon
Dental floss
Smock

ADULT PREPARATION:

1. Copy and trace tooth pattern on brown construction paper.
2. Cut out one tooth for each child.
3. Fold tooth cut-out in half, lengthwise.
4. Write child's name on the outside of the tooth with a marker.
5. Pour white tempera paint onto foam plate.
6. Add a quarter-size squirt of dish soap. Mix well with a spoon.
7. Cut an 8" piece of dental floss per child.

PROCEDURES:

The child will complete the following steps:

1. Put on smock.
2. Open tooth cut-out.

continued

Floss Your Teeth continued

3. Dip piece of dental floss into the white tempera paint.
4. Lay dental floss on one side of the tooth cutout.
5. Refold tooth cutout.
6. Place one hand on top of the folded cut-out.
7. Pull dental floss with the other hand until it is removed from the cut-out.
8. Open the tooth and observe the trail of paint left by the floss.
9. Repeat steps 3–8.

NOTE:

Attach a snap clothespin to the end of the floss to help younger children grip and pull the floss out of the tooth.

DISCUSSION SUGGESTIONS:

✂ People should use dental floss to clean between their teeth every day.
✂ Dental floss reaches parts of the tooth that a toothbrush cannot reach.

Food Match

ADULT PREPARATION:

1. Ask families to send in food labels with pictures of items that their child is familiar with. Send in duplicates if possible.
2. Trim labels with scissors.
3. Glue labels on squares of construction paper with rubber cement.
4. Lay labels face up.

PROCEDURES:

The child will complete the following steps:
1. Identify food on one label.
2. Look for matching label and place both together.
3. Repeat steps 1–2 until all matches have been found.

NOTE:

Start with 3 or 4 matching sets of labels for two-year-olds and add more labels as the child's skill level increases.

DISCUSSION SUGGESTIONS:

- ✂ As children identify the food products, ask them what type of food it is.
- ✂ Is the food healthy?
- ✂ What food group does the food belong with?

EXPANSION:

Older children may classify types of foods rather than identify identical matches, and may not need duplicate labels (i.e., when sorting the same type of food, different brands will be OK).

AGES: 2½–5

GROUP SIZE:

2–5 children

DEVELOPMENTAL GOALS:

- ✂ To develop one-to-one correspondence
- ✂ To enhance matching skills

LEARNING OBJECTIVE:

Using duplicate food labels, the child will match identical items.

MATERIALS:

Duplicate food labels
Scissors
Construction paper
Rubber cement

Galloping Game

GROUP SIZE:

6–12 children

DEVELOPMENTAL GOALS:

✂ To develop large muscles

✂ To practice coordination and balance

LEARNING OBJECTIVE:

Using a *stick horse* and chairs, the child will gallop around an obstacle course.

MATERIALS:

Horse head pattern (Appendix A11)
Copy paper
Markers
Scissors
Brown construction paper
Hole punch
Yarn
Black construction paper
Glue
Newspaper
Stapler and staples
Chairs

ADULT PREPARATION:

1. Copy, trace, and cut out a horse head from brown construction paper. Make two for each child.

2. Punch approximately six holes in the top of the horse's head.

3. Cut and tie yarn securely through each hole, creating a mane.

4. Cut circles out of black construction paper. Glue the circle on each side of the horse's head.

5. Roll several sheets of newspaper tightly.

6. Staple together two horse heads to the top of the newspaper roll, securing the roll to the heads and thus creating a *stick horse*.

7. Set chairs up in a large circle, at least four feet apart.

continued

Galloping Game continued

PROCEDURES:

The child will complete the following steps:

1. Mount the *stick horse.*
2. Gallop around the outside of the chairs in a large circle.
3. Gallop weaving in and out of the chairs.

NOTES:

✂ All children must move in the same direction to prevent collisions.

✂ This activity may be done inside or outside.

DISCUSSION SUGGESTIONS:

✂ Galloping is a form of exercise that strengthens the heart.

✂ When the heart beats faster, it is called cardiovascular exercise.

BOOK SUGGESTION:

The Galloping Book by Orli Zuravicky (New York: The Rosen Publishing Group, Inc., 2004). In both English and Spanish, photographs show children galloping in different ways.

G

AGES: 2½–5

GROUP SIZE:

2–5 children

DEVELOPMENTAL GOALS:

✄ To develop fine motor control

✄ To follow directions

LEARNING OBJECTIVE:

Using ground beef, elbow macaroni, spaghetti sauce, tablespoon, bowl, and a foil muffin liner, the child will follow directions to create a nutritious snack.

MATERIALS:

Long-handled spoon
Ground beef
Skillet
Colander
Water
Bowls
Pot
Elbow macaroni
Spaghetti sauce
Permanent marker
Jumbo foil muffin liners
Tablespoons
Baking sheet

Grand Goulash

ADULT PREPARATION:

1. Wash hands.
2. Brown ground beef and pour into colander.
3. Run hot water over the beef to rinse away excess fat.
4. Put ground beef in a bowl.
5. Wash colander and set it aside to use again.
6. Boil water in a pot and cook elbow macaroni according to the package directions.
7. Drain water from macaroni with a colander.
8. Put macaroni and spaghetti sauce into separate bowls.
9. Write each child's name on the bottom of a jumbo foil muffin liner.
10. Remove paper insert from the foil muffin liner.
11. Preheat the oven to 350°.

PROCEDURES:

The child will complete the following steps:

1. Wash hands.
2. Measure the following ingredients into a bowl and mix well:
   a. 2 tablespoons ground beef
   b. 2 tablespoons elbow macaroni
   c. 1–2 tablespoons spaghetti sauce
3. Select the muffin liner with his or her name.

The adult will complete the following steps:

1. Assist child in spooning their goulash into their muffin liner.
2. Place the muffin liner on the baking sheet.
3. Once the baking sheet is full, bake the individual servings of grand goulash for 10–12 minutes until heated.

VEGETARIAN SUBSTITUTION:

Use meatless ground burger and meatless spaghetti sauce.

32

Hair Care

AGES: 2½–5

GROUP SIZE:
2–6 children

DEVELOPMENTAL GOALS:

✂ To promote self-help skills

✂ To encourage healthy habits

LEARNING OBJECTIVE:

Using a large-tooth comb, cordless hair dryer, dishpan, bath towel, and empty shampoo and conditioner bottles, the child will practice taking care of his or her hair.

MATERIALS:

Empty plastic shampoo and conditioner bottles
Permanent marker
Large-tooth combs
Hair dryer with cord removed
Dishpan
Towel

ADULT PREPARATION:

1. Rinse shampoo and conditioner bottles to remove all product residue.
2. Write child's name with permanent marker on individual large-tooth combs.
3. Place comb, hair dryer, and shampoo and conditioner bottles in the dishpan.
4. Cover the dishpan with a towel.

PROCEDURES:

The child will complete the following steps:

1. Sit in a circle or semicircle for group time.
2. Listen to adult say, "I have some things hiding in this dishpan that help people take care of their hair. What do you think they are?"
3. Guess what is in the dishpan.
4. Identify each individual item the adult pulls out of the dishpan.
5. Tell how each hair care item is used.
6. Move the dishpan of hair care items to dramatic play area.
7. Take turns using the items.
8. Use the dishpan to pretend to wash hair.
9. Use only the comb with his or her name written on it.

continued

Hair Care continued

NOTE:

Individual combs may be sent home with the child. If kept at school, soak combs in a solution of one tablespoon bleach and one quart water. Allow to air dry before storing.

DISCUSSION SUGGESTIONS:

- ✂ Taking care of your hair keeps it healthy.
- ✂ Where do you wash your hair?
- ✂ Who helps you care for your hair?

BOOK SUGGESTION:

I Love My Hair! By Natasha Anastasia Tarpley (Boston: Little, Boston and Company, 1998). A young girl explores different ways she can style her hair.

Heartbeat

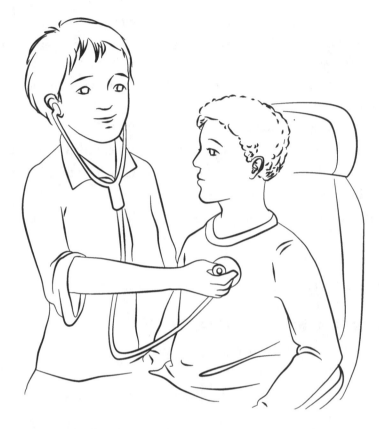

AGES: 4–5

GROUP SIZE:

1 child per adult and stethoscope

DEVELOPMENTAL GOALS:

- ✂ To encourage listening skills
- ✂ To develop counting skills

LEARNING OBJECTIVE:

Using a stethoscope, the child will listen and count the beats of his or her heart.

MATERIALS:

Stethoscope
Alcohol wipes or cotton balls and alcohol
Stopwatch or watch with second hand

ADULT PREPARATION:

1. Practice listening to own heartbeat to ensure he or she can find the heartbeat.
2. Wipe ear pieces of the stethoscope with an alcohol wipe, or use a cotton ball with alcohol.

PROCEDURES:

The child will complete the following steps:

1. Allow the adult to place the stethoscope in his or her ears while placing the other end on the adult's heart.
2. Tell adult whether or not they hear a heartbeat.
3. If a heartbeat is not heard, reposition the end of the stethoscope and try again.
4. Once a heartbeat is heard, the end of the stethoscope is transferred to the child's heart.

continued

Heartbeat continued

5. Tell adult whether or not they hear his or her own heartbeat.

6. If a heartbeat is not heard, reposition the end of the stethoscope and try again.

7. Count how many times his or her heart beats while the adult times the activity for 15 seconds.

8. Run in place while helping the adult count to 20.

9. Listen to his or her heartbeat again and time it for 15 seconds.

10. Answer the question, "What is the difference in your heartbeat?"

The adult will complete the following step:

1. Clean ear pieces of stethoscope with alcohol after each child.

NOTE:

The child's heartbeat should be faster after running.

DISCUSSION SUGGESTION:

✄ Exercise is a healthy habit.

✄ It helps the heart grow stronger.

✄ During exercise, the number of times a person's heart beats should increase.

EXPANSION:

Make a bar graph of the number of times the child's heart beats before and after running.

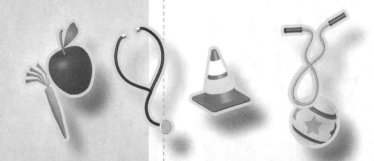

Helmet Match

ADULT PREPARATION:

1. Using newspapers, magazines, or the Internet, find pictures of helmets for various needs: bikes, football, baseball, skateboards, and motorcycles.
2. Cut the pictures out and glue them on construction paper squares.

PROCEDURES:

The child will complete the following steps:

1. Answer the questions, "Why are helmets used?" and "When are helmets used?"
2. Identify the colors of helmets.
3. Sort the helmets by color.

NOTE:

Start with only 3–4 colors for two-year-olds, and increase the number as the children's skill level increases.

DISCUSSION SUGGESTIONS:

- ✂ It is important to wear a helmet to keep a person's head safe when they are moving very quickly. You should wear a helmet when riding a bike, skateboard, roller skates, or a motorcycle.
- ✂ Many states have laws about wearing helmets when riding a bike or motorcycle.
- ✂ Check to see if your state requires helmets.

EXPANSION:

Older children may sort the helmets by categories (e.g., football, baseball, skateboards, bikes, motorcycles).

AGES: 2½–5

GROUP SIZE:
2–5 children

DEVELOPMENTAL GOALS:
- ✂ To develop visual discrimination
- ✂ To identify colors

LEARNING OBJECTIVE:
Using cutouts of various helmets the child will classify objects.

MATERIALS:
Newspapers
Magazines
Internet pictures
Scissors
Rubber cement
Construction paper

Huge Hero Sandwich

AGES: 2½–5

GROUP SIZE:

2–6 children

DEVELOPMENTAL GOALS:

✂ To follow directions

✂ To encourage social development through taking turns

LEARNING OBJECTIVE:

Using French bread, deli meat, sliced cheese, mayonnaise, mustard, lettuce, tomato, and a plastic knife, the children will follow directions to make a group sandwich.

MATERIALS:

Aluminum foil
Lettuce
Tomato
Serrated knife
Plates
Long loaf of French bread
Permanent marker
Mayonnaise
Mustard
Bowls
Deli meat
Sliced cheese
Plastic knives

ADULT PREPARATION:

1. Wash hands.
2. Cover the work area with aluminum foil.
3. Wash the lettuce and tomato.
4. Slice tomato with a serrated knife and place on a plate.
5. Tear pieces of lettuce and put on a plate.
6. Use the serrated knife to cut the French bread in half, lengthwise.
7. Set the open bread on the foil.
8. Use the permanent marker to write each child's name below an equal section of the bread.
9. Place mayonnaise and mustard in separate bowls.
10. Place sliced meat and cheese on separate plates.
11. Label plates with each child's name.

PROCEDURES:

The children will complete the following steps:

1. Wash hands.
2. Take turns in front of his or her section of the bread.

continued

Huge Hero Sandwich continued

3. Use a plastic knife to spread mayonnaise and/or mustard on the bread.
4. Select lettuce, cheese, tomato, and/or meat to place on his or her section of bread.

The adult will complete the following steps:

1. Close top of bread over the huge hero sandwich.
2. Show children the huge sandwich.
3. Use the serrated knife to slice each section of the sandwich and put them on the children's labeled plates.

DISCUSSION SUGGESTIONS:

✄ A hero sandwich contains healthy food from the meat, dairy, vegetable, fruit, and grain groups.

✄ Have children identify which food belongs to each group. (Hint: The tomato is a fruit.)

VEGETARIAN SUBSTITUTION:

Omit the deli meat.

DAIRY ALLERGIES:

For a child who is allergic to dairy or lactose intolerant, either leave the cheese off one section or ask the parent to bring in a vegetable cheese slice.

Identification Card

AGES: 2½–5

GROUP SIZE:

2–5 children

DEVELOPMENTAL GOALS:

✄ To promote safety

✄ To follow directions

LEARNING OBJECTIVE:

Using an identification form and picture, the child will create an identification card.

MATERIALS:

Permission form to be photographed and videotaped (Appendix B7)
Camera with film or a digital camera
Pen
Copy paper
Card stock paper
Identification form (Appendix B9)
Adult scissors
Child safety scissors
Glue
Clear contact paper

ADULT PREPARATION:

1. Take a picture of each child and develop or print them.
2. Make a list of each child's full name, address, phone number, and birth date.
3. Make a copy of the identification form for each child on card stock paper.
4. Trim the edges of the paper.
5. Cut each child's picture to fit the space on the identification form.

PROCEDURES:

The child will complete the following steps:

1. Tell adult his or her name, address, phone number, and birth date as the adult writes it down on child's identification form. Adult may aid child if information is incorrect or incomplete.

continued

Identification Card continued

2. Glue his or her picture in the appropriate space on the identification form.
3. Assist adult in covering the identification form with clear contact paper on the front and back.
4. Trim the edges of the contact paper with safety scissors.

NOTES:

✂ Make sure there is a copy of the permissions form on file for each child to be photographed.

✂ Older children may copy their own identifying information onto the card if the form is full size.

DISCUSSION SUGGESTIONS:

✂ Photo-IDs help keep people safe.

✂ If a person is lost, identification can help find the way home.

Indian Bread

AGES: 3–5

GROUP SIZE:

2–5 children

DEVELOPMENTAL GOALS:

✂ To develop hand muscles

✂ To promote nutritional practices

LEARNING OBJECTIVE:

Using frozen bread dough, a child-size rolling pin, flour, a foam plate, plastic knife, tablespoon, honey, and a spoon, the child will make Indian bread.

MATERIALS:

Frozen bread dough
Flour
Bowl
Knife
Foam plate
Vegetable oil
Electric skillet
Tablespoon
Child-size rolling pin
Plastic knife
Tongs
Paper towels
Honey
Spoon

ADULT PREPARATION:

1. Place bread dough in refrigerator overnight to thaw.
2. Wash hands.
3. Place flour in a bowl.
4. Cut dough into equal portions.
5. Place dough pieces on a foam plate.
6. Place vegetable oil in a skillet.

PROCEDURES:

The child will complete the following steps:

1. Wash hands.
2. Spread 1 tablespoon of flour on a foam plate.
3. Select a portion of dough.
4. Use the child-size rolling pin to flatten the dough to approximately ½" thick.
5. Cut the dough into squares.

The adult will complete the following steps:

1. Take the dough to the kitchen.
2. Heat the skillet to approximately 375°.
3. Place the dough in the skillet.
4. When one side is golden brown, carefully turn the dough over with the tongs.
5. When both sides are golden brown, remove the bread from the skillet and drain on paper towels.
6. Place the dough on individual plates.
7. Place honey in a bowl with a spoon.

The child will complete the following steps:

1. Wash hands.
2. Drizzle honey on the bread.

continued

Indian Bread continued

DISCUSSION SUGGESTIONS:

- ✂ Bread is from the grain group.
- ✂ Depending upon a person's age and amount of daily exercise, a child between the ages of 2 and 8 needs between 3 and 5 ounce equivalents daily.
- ✂ An ounce equivalent may be one slice of bread, ½ cup of pasta, or ½ cup of cereal.
- ✂ Check http://www.mypyramid.gov for more information.

Isometric Exercise

AGES: 4–5

GROUP SIZE:

4–8 children

DEVELOPMENTAL GOALS:

✂ To strengthen muscles

✂ To develop concentration

LEARNING OBJECTIVE:

Using long scarves, the children will do a resistance exercise.

MATERIALS:

Long scarf (one for each child)

ADULT PREPARATION:

1. Clear a carpeted area for exercise.

PROCEDURES:

The children will complete the following steps:

1. Hold one end of the scarf in each hand.
2. Put feet in the center of the scarf and straighten legs so the scarf is on the bottom of the feet.
3. Lay on back with hands still holding scarf.

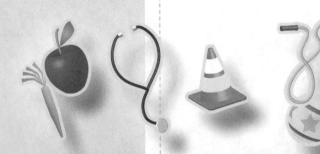

continued

Isometric Exercise continued

4. Pull scarf to straighten to a sitting position.
5. Hold for the count of 10.
6. Lay back down and repeat steps 4–5.

NOTE:

Adult may need to demonstrate this exercise first.

DISCUSSION SUGGESTIONS:

✂ Isometric exercises help build healthy muscles.

✂ This type of exercise is called "resistance training," which is an important part of an exercise program.

✂ Resistance training builds muscles that continue to burn calories even when a person is resting.

J

Jogging

AGES: 2–5

GROUP SIZE:

4–16 children

DEVELOPMENTAL GOALS:

✄ To stimulate physical development

✄ To enhance large muscle coordination

LEARNING OBJECTIVE:

Using directions from an adult, the children will use large muscles as they jog.

MATERIALS:

None needed

ADULT PREPARATION:

1. Clear large area for jogging.

PROCEDURES:

The children will complete the following steps:

1. Listen to adult explain, "When we run, we go very, very fast. Today we are going to jog. Jogging is like running, but we go at a slow, steady pace."

2. Form a line behind the adult.

continued

Jogging continued

3. Follow the adult in a slow, steady jog.

4. Stop. The adult will go to the end of the line, and the first child will lead the group in a slow, steady jog.

5. Stop. The first child will go to the end of the line, and the second child will lead the group in a slow, steady jog.

6. Repeat step 5 until all children have had a turn to lead the group.

NOTE:

If a child is physically unable to jog, he or she could manage the group by giving "stop" and "go" directions.

DISCUSSION SUGGESTIONS:

✁ Jogging is a healthy exercise, but it must be done in a safe place.

✁ To be safe, where would you jog?

✁ Who would you jog with?

J

GROUP SIZE:

4–16 children

DEVELOPMENTAL GOALS:

✂ To develop number skills

✂ To promote large muscle development

LEARNING OBJECTIVE:

Using number cards, the children will recognize the number and jump the amount given.

MATERIALS:

Construction paper
Scissors
Marker
Basket

Jumping

ADULT PREPARATION:

1. Cut construction paper into squares.
2. Write the numbers on the squares depending upon the child's age and ability to recognize numbers.
   a. Two-year-olds (0–5)
   b. Three-year-olds (0–10)
   c. Four-year-olds (0–12)
   d. Five-year-olds (0–20)
3. Mix up the cards and place them in a basket.

NOTE:

For younger children, dots may be added to the cards to assist the child in counting.

PROCEDURES:

The children will complete the following steps:

1. Stand in a circle, approximately 3–4 feet apart.
2. One child will select a number card out of the basket.
3. Show the group the card.
4. The group will identify the number on the card and jump that number of times.
5. Steps 2–4 will be repeated until all children have had an opportunity to draw a number card.

DISCUSSION SUGGESTIONS:

✂ Jumping is a healthy activity that strengthens the muscles in the legs.

✂ Jumping also strengthens the heart.

48

Junk Food Jingle

GROUP SIZE:
4–20 children

DEVELOPMENTAL GOALS:

✂ To understand the difference between healthy food and nonhealthy food

✂ To create a feeling of well-being through music

LEARNING OBJECTIVE:

Using a song poster and pictures of healthy and nonhealthy food, the children will sing a song.

MATERIALS:

Poster board
Markers
Magazines with pictures of food
Scissors
Rubber cement

ADULT PREPARATION:

1. Write the words to *Junk Food Jingle* on poster board.
2. Cut pictures of food out of magazines.
3. Mount them on the poster board with rubber cement.

PROCEDURES:

The children will complete the following steps:

1. Identify the food on the song board.
2. Classify the food as healthy or junk food.
3. Sing the following song to the tune of *Mary Had a Little Lamb*:
   Junk Food Jingle

Junk food is not good for us,

It doesn't help us grow,

Foods like candy, chips, and soda,

Should be limited we know.

continued

Junk Food Jingle continued

Protein and grains are good for us,
They help the body grow,
Foods like eggs, bread, and nuts,
Will help our body grow.

Junk food is not good for us,
It doesn't help us grow,
Foods like cakes and cookies,
Should be limited we know.

Vegetables are good for us,
They help the body grow,
Foods like carrots, peas, and corn,
Will help our body grow.

Junk food is not good for us,
It doesn't help us grow,
Foods like candy, chips, and soda,
Should be limited we know.

Fruit and milk are good for us,
They help the body grow,
Foods like apples, pears, and milk,
Will help our body grow.

Junk food is not good for us,
It doesn't help us grow,
Foods like cakes and cookies,
Should be limited we know.

NOTE:

A rebus song board could be made with pictures of food substituting for the words.

continued

Junk Food Jingle continued

DISCUSSION SUGGESTIONS:

- ✂ A small amount of junk food may taste good.
- ✂ Eating a lot of junk food is not healthy. It may make a person feel sick or have an upset stomach.
- ✂ Eating too much food that is not healthy may cause a person to feel full and not have room for healthy food.

Kettle of Kidney Beans

AGES: 2–5

GROUP SIZE:

4–6 children

DEVELOPMENTAL GOALS:

✄ To develop small muscles

✄ To promote social development

LEARNING OBJECTIVE:

Using kidney beans, onions, tomato sauce, salt, pepper, spoons, and a pot, the children will cook together.

MATERIALS:

Olive oil
Tablespoon
Pot with lid
Knife
Onion
Bowls
Smooth-edge can opener
15 oz. can kidney beans
15 oz. can tomato sauce
Salt
Pepper
Large pot
Long-handled spoon
Spoons

ADULT PREPARATION:

1. Wash hands.
2. Place 1 tablespoon olive oil in a pot. Turn the stove on medium-high.
3. Chop the onion and add to the oil.
4. Sauté the onion until soft, remove the pot from the heat, and then pour the onion into a bowl.
5. Open the kidney beans and pour them into a bowl.
6. Open the tomato sauce and pour it into a bowl.
7. Pour salt and pepper into separate bowls.
8. Rinse the pot with cold water or use a second pot to put on the table.

PROCEDURES:

The children will complete the following steps:
1. Wash hands.
2. Take turns adding the following ingredients to the pot:
   a. The chopped onion
   b. 15 oz. of kidney beans
   c. 15 oz. tomato sauce
   d. Pinch of salt
   e. Pinch of pepper
3. Take turns stirring the kidney bean mixture.

The adult will complete the following steps:
1. Take pot to the kitchen and place on the stove.
2. Cook the ingredients on medium-high until they come to a boil.
3. Cover and simmer for 20 minutes.
4. Spoon into bowls for children to eat.

continued

Kettle of Kidney Beans continued

DISCUSSION SUGGESTIONS:

✄ Kidney beans are a healthy selection from the meat and bean group.

✄ Children ages 2–8 should eat 2 to 4 ounce equivalents from this group daily, depending upon their age and the amount of exercise they get.

✄ ¼ cup of cooked kidney beans is considered as 1 ounce equivalent.

✄ See http://www.mypyramid.gov for more information.

Knee Bend Polka

AGES: 2¹⁄₂–5

GROUP SIZE:

4–16 children

DEVELOPMENTAL GOALS:

✂ To combine music with movement

✂ To develop large muscles

LEARNING OBJECTIVE:

Using a song board, the children will participate in a large muscle movement activity.

MATERIALS:

Poster board
Markers
Masking tape

ADULT PREPARATION:

1. Write the words to *Knee Bend Polka* on the poster board.
2. Place the song board on the wall at the children's eye level with masking tape.
3. Clear a large area for movement.

PROCEDURES:

The children will complete the following steps:

1. Stand in a large circle, approximately 4 feet apart.
2. Sing the following song, doing the actions in the song to the tune of *Hokey Pokey.*

Knee Bend Polka

Let your knees bend down.

Let your knees straighten up.

Let your knees bend down,

continued

Knee Bend Polka continued

And shake them all about.

Do the knee bend polka

As you turn yourself around,

Now sit on the ground.

(While sitting on the ground continue the song with legs stretched out straight.)

Let your knees bend up.

Let your knees straighten out.

Let your knees bend up,

And shake them all about.

Do the knee bend polka,

And move to the beat.

Now stand up on your feet.

3. Repeat verses.

DISCUSSION SUGGESTIONS:

✂ It is important to exercise all areas of the body to stay healthy.

✂ Bending the knees strengthens the muscles that support them.

Knife Handling Safety

AGES: 3–5

GROUP SIZE:

2–3 children

DEVELOPMENTAL GOALS:

- ✂ To enhance fine motor control
- ✂ To practice safety

LEARNING OBJECTIVE:

Using bread, peanut butter, honey, table knives, and plates, the child will practice spreading and cutting with a knife.

MATERIALS:

Bread
Table knives
Paper plates
Peanut butter
Honey
Bowls
Spoons
Permanent marker

ADULT PREPARATION:

1. Wash hands.
2. Cut bread slices in half.
3. Place bread on plate.
4. Put peanut butter and honey in separate bowls.
5. Place a spoon in each bowl.
6. Write children's names on paper plates.

PROCEDURES:

The child will complete the following steps:

1. Watch the adult show how to hold the knife, how to pass the knife, how to spread, how to cut, and to keep the knife away from the face (mouth).
2. Select the plate with his or her name.
3. Take two half pieces of bread and place on the plate.
4. Place peanut butter onto one half of bread.

continued

Knife Handling Safety continued

5. Spread the peanut butter with the table knife.
6. Spoon honey onto the other half of bread.
7. Spread the honey with the table knife.
8. Place one half of bread on top of other half.
9. Cut the sandwich in half.

NOTE:

Older children may have two whole slices of bread, and then cut their sandwich into quarters.

DISCUSSION SUGGESTIONS:

✄ As children grow older, they need experience handling knives safely.

✄ Knives are used for spreading and cutting.

✄ Knives are held only by the handle.

✄ The sharp edge of the knife is always turned down.

✄ With older children, the adult will want to demonstrate how to pass a knife. (Hold the top of the handle and extend the bottom of the handle for the person to hold.)

 ## SAFETY PRECAUTION:

If a child is allergic to nuts, omit the peanut butter.

Laughter Lyrics

L

AGES: 3–5

GROUP SIZE:

4–14 children

DEVELOPMENTAL GOALS:

✄ To encourage social development

✄ To promote a feeling of well-being

LEARNING OBJECTIVE:

Using a poster board with the words written on it, the children will chant the laughter lyrics.

MATERIALS:

Poster board
Marker

ADULT PREPARATION:

1. Write the words to *Laughter Lyrics* on the poster board.

PROCEDURES:

The children will complete the following steps:

1. The children will sit in a semicircle, facing the poster board.
2. The children will chant the following lyrics:

Laughter Lyrics

When we laugh, we laugh out loud,

We feel so good, we're in a cloud.

We laugh and laugh and cannot stop,

We feel just like a spinning top.

When we laugh, we laugh out loud.

DISCUSSION SUGGESTION:

✄ Laughter creates endorphins in a person's body.

✄ Endorphins cause people to feel good.

✄ This feeling can "have a calming effect for hours" (Dacey & Fiore, 2000, p. 71).

Leeks

ADULT PREPARATION:

1. Wash hands.
2. Wash potatoes and carrots and place them on a cutting board. Peel and chop them, then place them in separate bowls.
3. Cut the leeks in half. Wash well.
4. Cut the roots away from the leeks.
5. Cut the leeks, including the green stalk. Put the pieces in a separate bowl.
6. Pour vegetable broth in a bowl that the children will be able to scoop a ¼-cup measure into.

PROCEDURES:

The children will complete the following steps:

1. Wash hands.
2. Each child will add the following ingredients to the pot:
   a. ¼ cup chopped leeks
   b. ¼ cup chopped carrots
   c. ¼ cup chopped potatoes
   d. ¼ cup vegetable broth

The adult will complete the following steps:

1. If broth doesn't cover vegetables, add more until it does.
2. Put the pot on the stove on high heat. Bring to a boil.
3. Stir ingredients and reduce heat to simmer for 20 minutes.
4. Once all the vegetables are tender, turn off heat.
5. Mash the vegetables with the potato masher to make a thicker broth.
6. Optional: Add salt.

DISCUSSION SUGGESTIONS:

- ✄ Leeks are a nutritious vegetable.
- ✄ Leeks contain potassium and folic acid.

AGES: 3–5

GROUP SIZE:
4–12 children

DEVELOPMENTAL GOALS:
- ✄ To develop self-help skills
- ✄ To develop an understanding of nutrition

LEARNING OBJECTIVE:
Using leeks, carrots, potatoes, measuring cups, and vegetable broth, the children will create a soup.

MATERIALS:
Potatoes
Carrots
Vegetable peeler
Paring knife
Cutting board
Bowls
Leeks
Vegetable broth
Measuring cups
Large pot
Potato masher
Salt (optional)

Life Jackets

L

AGES: 3–5
- - - - - - - - - - - - -

GROUP SIZE:

2–4 depending upon
the size of the box

DEVELOPMENTAL GOALS:

✂ To understand the
need for life jackets

✂ To practice role
playing

LEARNING OBJECTIVE:

Using a child-size life
jacket, large box, chairs,
and a steering wheel,
the child will practice
life jacket safety.

MATERIALS:

Utility knife
Large box
Empty paper towel
tube
Packing tape
Poster board
Scissors
Chairs
Child-size life jackets

ADULT PREPARATION:

1. Using a utility knife cut the lid off the box and cut a door into one
side of the box.

2. Cut a small hole in the front of the box. Insert the empty paper towel
tube in the hole. The tube should jut into the box. Using the packing
tape secure the tube.

3. Cut the poster board into a 12" circle to make a steering wheel. Cut a
smaller circle in the center of the wheel. Place the small circle over
the tube jutting into the box. Taping the circle is optional.

4. Place chairs in the box.

5. Place a life jacket on each chair.

PROCEDURES:

The child will complete the following steps:

1. Listen to adult explain, "When you ride in a boat, you must wear life
jackets."

2. Sit in the boat.

continued

Life Jackets continued

3. Place the life jacket on.
4. Pretend to drive the boat.
5. Repeat steps 2–4 until each child has had a turn.

DISCUSSION SUGGESTIONS:

✄ Life jackets keep people safe.

✄ Life jackets help people float in the water.

✄ It is important to wear a life jacket when on a boat.

✄ Young children should also wear a life jacket when walking on a dock or near water.

✄ Even when wearing a life jacket, a child should not be alone when near water.

Mask Safety

AGES: 2¹/₂–5

GROUP SIZE:

2–6 children

DEVELOPMENTAL GOALS:

- ✂ To promote creativity
- ✂ To recognize safe objects

LEARNING OBJECTIVE:

Using a paper plate, craft stick, tempera paint, soap, paint brush, and markers, the child will create a safe mask.

MATERIALS:

Scissors
Paper plate
Stapler and staples
Craft stick
Tempera paint
Container
Dish soap
Paint brush

ADULT PREPARATION:

1. Cut paper plate in half.
2. Cut holes for eyes.
3. Staple craft stick on the right side of the plate on the back.
4. Pour tempera paint into a container. Mix with 1–2 tablespoons of dish soap.

PROCEDURES:

The child will complete the following steps:

1. Listen to adult explain, "In order to wear the mask safely, you must be able to see well through the eye openings."
2. Hold the mask up to his or her face.
3. If the eye holes are not large enough, the adult needs to cut them again.
4. Once the eye holes are safe, color or paint mask to decorate.

DISCUSSION SUGGESTIONS:

- ✂ Why is it important for the eye holes in a mask to be large?
- ✂ In order to be safe, a child must be able to see well when wearing a mask.
- ✂ When doing a lot of walking, it may be safer to paint a child's face instead of wearing a mask.

Melon Salad

AGES: 3–5

GROUP SIZE:

2–6 children

DEVELOPMENTAL GOALS:

✂ To develop counting skills

✂ To promote self-help skills

LEARNING OBJECTIVE:

Using cantaloupe, honeydew melon, watermelon, yogurt, melon scooper, tablespoon, and bowls, the child will make their own melon salad.

MATERIALS:

Watermelon
Cantaloupe
Honeydew melon
Knife
Tablespoon
Plates
Yogurt
Permanent marker
Foam bowls
Melon scooper

ADULT PREPARATION:

1. Wash hands.
2. Wash and slice the melons in half and remove seeds.
3. Place the melon halves on separate plates.
4. Pour yogurt into a bowl.
5. Write child's name on the bottom of the bowl.

PROCEDURES:

The child will complete the following steps:

1. Wash hands.
2. Choose bowl with his or her name on the bottom.
3. Using the melon scoop, choose a melon and place two scoops in a bowl. Count the scoops as they are placed in the bowl.
4. Repeat step 3 with the second and third melon.
5. Count the total of six melon scoops.
6. Place two tablespoons of yogurt over the melon and stir.

continued

Melon Salad continued

DISCUSSION SUGGESTIONS:

- ✄ Fruit is a nutritious snack.
- ✄ Watermelon, cantaloupe, and honeydew are all fruits that are melons.
- ✄ Six melon balls, or about 1 cup of melon, would be the amount of fruit a two- to three-year-old needs daily.
- ✄ A four- to eight-year-old needs 1–1½ cups of fruit daily.

Nine-One-One

AGES: 3–5

GROUP SIZE:

2 children

DEVELOPMENTAL GOALS:

✄ To promote an awareness of safety procedures

✄ To develop self-help skills

LEARNING OBJECTIVE:

Using a telephone and number card, the child will dial 911.

MATERIALS:

Marker
Index card
Telephone

ADULT PREPARATION:

1. Write *911* on an index card.

PROCEDURES:

The child will complete the following steps:

1. Look at index card and identify the numbers.
2. Answer the question, "When do we use those numbers?"
3. Practice calling 911 to report an emergency.
4. Report the emergency to the operator. Adult may need to guide child through what to say.
5. Give operator information such as the phone number calling from and address. Adult may need to guide child through this information.

DISCUSSION SUGGESTIONS:

✄ When would you call 911?

✄ What would you tell the 911 operator?

BOOK SUGGESTION:

Little Flower by Gloria Rand. (New York: Henry Holt and Company, 2002). Miss Pearl's potbellied pig, Little Flower, comes to her rescue until someone calls 911 for help.

Noise That Is Loud

AGES: 2¹/₂–5

GROUP SIZE:

4–20 children

DEVELOPMENTAL GOALS:

✄ To recognize differences in volume

✄ To participate in a group experience

LEARNING OBJECTIVE:

Using a song board, the children will sing a song about noise.

MATERIALS:

Poster board
Markers
Masking tape

ADULT PREPARATION:

1. Write the words to *Noise That Is Loud* on poster board.
2. Tape the song board to the wall at the child's eye level.

PROCEDURES:

The children will complete the following step:

1. Sing *Noise That is Loud* to the tune of *Itsy Bitsy Spider* while doing the appropriate motions.

Noise That Is Loud

Noise that is loud can hurt my head and ears.	*(Sing loudly and cover ears with hands)*
It makes me scared and breaks some down to tears.	*(Rub eyes)*
We need it quiet so turn the volume down.	*(Sing softly and pretend to turn knob)*
And can think much better without that loud sound.	*(Hands out, palms up)*

NOTE:

This song may be sung at various times throughout the day as the need for quiet times mandate.

DISCUSSION SUGGESTIONS:

✄ Constantly being around noise can be harmful.

✄ Noise is associated with higher blood pressure.

✄ Noise may affect the ability to pay attention.

✄ Noise can affect reading and language skills.

BOOK SUGGESTION:

Noisy Nora by Rosemary Wells (New York: Dial Books for Young Readers, 1973). Nora constantly makes noise for attention. When it suddenly becomes quiet, her family becomes concerned.

Nutritious Nest

AGES: 3–5

GROUP SIZE:

2–5 children

DEVELOPMENTAL GOALS:

✄ To practice measuring

✄ To make a nutritious snack

LEARNING OBJECTIVE:

Using rice, egg substitute, carrots, zucchini, margarine or butter, measuring spoons, a bowl, spoon, and foil muffin liners, the child will measure ingredients and make a nutritious snack.

MATERIALS:

Pot
Rice
Water
Zucchini
Carrots
Vegetable peeler
Grater
Spoons
Bowls
Margarine or butter

ADULT PREPARATION:

1. Wash hands.
2. Boil rice according to package directions.
3. Wash and peel zucchini and carrots.
4. Shred vegetables and mix them together in a bowl.
5. Place softened margarine or butter in a bowl.
6. Write children's names on the bottom of the foil muffin liners.
7. Remove the paper insert from the liners.
8. Preheat the oven to 350°.

PROCEDURES:

The child will complete the following steps:

1. Wash hands.

continued

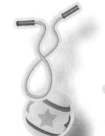

Nutritious Nest continued

MATERIALS:

Permanent marker
Foil muffin liner
Measuring spoons
Egg substitute
Salt
Baking sheet

2. Measure the following ingredients and mix well in a bowl:

    a. 2 tablespoons rice

    b. 1 teaspoon egg substitute

    c. Pinch of salt

3. Select muffin liner with his or her name.

4. Press rice mixture into sides and bottom of liner.

5. Measure and add 2 tablespoons of grated vegetables to the liner.

6. Measure and add ½ teaspoon of margarine or butter on top of the vegetables.

7. With adult assistance, move the nest to the baking sheet.

The adult will complete the following step:

1. Once the baking sheet is full, bake the nutritious nests for 20 minutes. The rice and egg mixture should be firm.

DISCUSSION SUGGESTIONS:

✂ The nutritious nest contains three different food groups.

✂ What foods are from the vegetable group?

✂ What food is from the grain group?

✂ What food is from the meat and bean group?

Oatmeal

ADULT PREPARATION:

1. Wash hands.
2. Place quick-cooking oatmeal, water, raisins, and cinnamon in separate bowls.
3. Wash, peel, core, and dice apples. Place in a bowl.

PROCEDURES:

The children will complete the following steps:

1. Wash hands.
2. Take turns each measuring the following ingredients into the pot:
   a. ⅛ cup of oatmeal
   b. ¼ cup of water
   c. 1 tablespoon diced apples
   d. 1 tablespoon raisins
   e. ⅛ teaspoon cinnamon
3. Take turns stirring the ingredients with a long-handled spoon.

The adult will complete the following steps:

1. Place the pot on the stove or hot plate.
2. Bring ingredients to a boil, then cover and simmer for 10 minutes.

⊘ SAFETY PRECAUTION:

When using small food items like raisins, supervise children closely to prevent choking.

DISCUSSION SUGGESTIONS:

- ✂ Oatmeal is a nutritious food from the grain group.
- ✂ A two- to three-year-old child need 3 ounce equivalents each day.
- ✂ Four- to eight-year-old children need 4–5 ounce equivalents each day.
- ✂ A half cup of oatmeal is 1 ounce equivalent.

EXPANSION:

Read a version of the story of the three bears and substitute porridge with oatmeal.

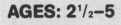

AGES: 2½–5

GROUP SIZE:
2–6 children

DEVELOPMENTAL GOALS:
- ✂ To encourage healthy eating habits
- ✂ To develop self-help skills

LEARNING OBJECTIVE:
Using quick-cooking oatmeal, water, apples, raisins, cinnamon, measuring spoons, and cups, a long-handled spoon, and a pot, the children will make a healthy snack.

MATERIALS:
Pot with lid
Quick-cooking oatmeal
Water
Raisins
Cinnamon
Bowls
Paring knife
Apple slicer/corer
Measuring spoons
Long-handled spoon

Optometrist

AGES: 3–5

GROUP SIZE:

4–16 children (group time) or 2 children (dramatic play)

DEVELOPMENTAL GOALS:

✄ To practice role-playing

✄ To promote social development

LEARNING OBJECTIVE:

Using glasses without lenses, an eye chart, an eye cover, a cash register, wallet, or coin purse, and play money, children will pretend to visit the optometrist.

MATERIALS:

Eye chart (Appendix A12)
Copy paper
Masking tape
Glasses without lenses
Pencil
Tag board
Scissors
Stapler and staples
Tongue depressor

ADULT PREPARATION:

1. Make two copies of the eye chart.
2. Tape one on the wall in the dramatic play area. Make sure to tape it at the children's eye level.
3. If glasses have lenses, remove them.
4. Display the glasses on the shelves or table.
5. Trace circles on the tag board approximately 3–4" in diameter.
6. Staple the circle to a tongue depressor. Make one for each child.
7. Write child's name on the circle.
8. Set the cash register on the table.
9. Put play money in the cash register and wallet.

PROCEDURES:

The children will complete the following steps:

1. Sit in a circle or semicircle for group time.
2. Look at the eye chart.
3. Discuss the letter E on the eye chart.
4. As the adult points to different Es, answer the question, "Which way does the E face?"

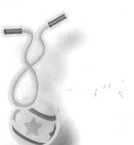

continued

Optometrist continued

5. Select a circle stapled to a tongue depressor with his or her name.

6. Hold by the stick and cover one eye with the circle.

7. Look at the eye chart again.

8. As the adult points to different Es, answer the question, "Which way does the E face?"

9. Repeat steps 6–8 covering the other eye.

10. Listen to the adult explain, "This is the way an optometrist checks eyes. Sometimes people find they need glasses to see well. Some optometrists will also fit people with glasses and sell them."

11. Take turns in dramatic play.

12. Assign roles of optometrist and customer.

13. The optometrist points to the Es on the chart and asks, "Which way does the E point?"

14. The customer then takes turns covering each eye and answers the same question.

15. If the optometrist decides the customer needs glasses, the customer may select a pair of glasses and pay for them with the money in the coin purse or wallet.

16. The optometrist rings up the sale and gives change.

DISCUSSION SUGGESTIONS:

✂ Why do people wear glasses?

✂ Some people need glasses to see far away. They are called near-sighted, because they can see things that are near.

✂ Some people need glasses to see things that are close. They are called farsighted, because they can see things that are far away.

MATERIALS:

Marker
Cash register
Play money
Coin purse or wallet

O

Oxygen

AGES: 4–5

GROUP SIZE:

6–12 children

DEVELOPMENTAL GOALS:

- ✂ To practice observation skills
- ✂ To increase vocabulary

LEARNING OBJECTIVE:

Using a lit candle and a glass jar with a lid, the children will observe the absence of oxygen.

MATERIALS:

Glass jar with lid
Tray
Candle (votive)
Lighter
Tray

ADULT PREPARATION:

1. Place jar and lid on tray.
2. Place candle on lid.

PROCEDURES:

The children will complete the following steps:

1. Children sit in a semicircle.
2. Answer the question, "What do we breathe?"
3. Listen to adult say, "Fire needs air or oxygen just like we do."
4. Watch adult light the candle and then place the glass jar upside down, onto the lid, over the candle. Fit the jar into the lid.

continued

Oxygen continued

5. Answer the question, "Why do only adults use lighters or matches?"

6. Answer the question, "What is happening to the candle?"

NOTE:

The fire will use up the oxygen from the jar, and the candle will slowly burn out.

Pharmacist

AGES: 3–5

GROUP SIZE:

2–3 children

DEVELOPMENTAL GOALS:

✄ To promote self-help skills

✄ To role-play life situations

LEARNING OBJECTIVE:

Using small plastic bottles with lids, beads, cash register, play money, wallet or coin purse, small bags, and a prescription pattern, the children will role-play a trip to the pharmacist.

MATERIALS:

Prescription pattern (Appendix A13)
Copy paper
Marker
Play money
Cash register
Wallet or coin purse
Small plastic bottles with lids
Small bags

ADULT PREPARATION:

1. Make copies of the prescription pattern.
2. Write children's names on prescription patterns.
3. Put play money in the cash register and wallet or coin purse.

PROCEDURES:

The children will complete the following steps:

1. Assign roles of customer and pharmacist.
2. The customer will find the prescription pattern with their name.
3. The customer will hand the pharmacist their prescription.
4. The pharmacist will ring up the price on the cash register.
5. The customer will pay the pharmacist.
6. The pharmacist will put a prescription bottle in the bag and hand it to the customer.
7. Steps 1–2 are repeated with children taking turns with different roles.

continued

Pharmacist continued

NOTE:

Ask the local pharmacist for blank prescription bags to use for the small bags. If none are available, use lunch bags.

DISCUSSION SUGGESTIONS:

✄ Who gives you medicine?

✄ When do you take medicine?

✄ Where does your medicine come from?

Protein

AGES: 2–5

GROUP SIZE:

2–4 children

DEVELOPMENTAL GOALS:

✄ To develop matching skills
✄ To identify foods with protein

LEARNING OBJECTIVE:

Using duplicate cards with pictures of protein-rich food, the child will practice matching.

MATERIALS:

Protein food cards
   (Appendix A14–A21):
   Peanut butter
   (Appendix A14)
   Dried beans
   (Appendix A15)
   Fish (Appendix A16)
   Chicken drumstick
   (Appendix A17)
   Pork chop
   (Appendix A18)
   Beef (Appendix A19)
   Egg (Appendix A20)
   Nuts (Appendix A21)
Copy paper
Construction paper
Rubber cement
Scissors

ADULT PREPARATION:

1. Make duplicate copies of the protein food cards.
2. Cut construction paper into squares to fit the food cards.
3. Using rubber cement, glue the food cards to the construction paper squares.
4. Lay the protein food cards face down on the table in random order.

PROCEDURES:

The child will complete the following steps:

1. Turn two cards over at a time.
2. Identify the protein foods on the cards.
3. If the cards are the same, set them aside.
4. If the cards are different, turn them face down.
5. Repeat steps 1–4 until all matches are found.

NOTE:

Start with 3–4 matches (6–8 cards) for two-year-olds. As children age and their skill level increases, add more matching cards.

DISCUSSION SUGGESTIONS:

✄ Protein is found in the meat and bean group.
✄ Protein is needed to build muscles.
✄ Protein helps provide energy.

Pulse

AGES: 4–5

GROUP SIZE:
2–3 children

DEVELOPMENTAL GOALS:

✂ To stimulate cognitive development

✂ To promote the sense of touch

LEARNING OBJECTIVE:
Using his or her fingers, the child will find their pulse.

MATERIALS:
Heart pattern (Appendix A22)
Copy paper
Timer or watch with a second hand

ADULT PREPARATION:

1. Make a copy of the heart pattern.

PROCEDURES:

The child will complete the following steps:

1. Look at the heart pattern.
2. Listen to the adult explain that the heart pumps blood through the body and that this is felt through the pulse.

continued

Pulse continued

3. Using the tips of the index, middle, and ring fingers, the child will feel the carotid artery in the neck to feel their pulse. Adult assistance will be needed to first find the pulse.

4. Once the pulse is found, the adult will time the children for 10 seconds as they count their pulse.

The adult will complete the following step:

1. Multiply the child's pulse times six to achieve the child's heart rate.

EXPANSION:

Make a bar graph of the children's heart rates.

Pyramid Puzzle

AGES: 3–5

GROUP SIZE:
3–6 children

DEVELOPMENTAL GOALS:
✂ To recognize types of healthy food
✂ To develop fine motor skills

LEARNING OBJECTIVE:
Using the Food Guide Pyramid pattern and small pictures of food, the child will put a puzzle together.

MATERIALS:
Food Guide
  Pyramid pattern
  (Appendix A23)
Copy paper
Orange, green, red, yellow, blue, and purple crayons or markers
Rubber cement
Construction paper
Scissors
Magazines or advertisements with small pictures of food
Bowl
Glue

ADULT PREPARATION:

1. Make two copies of the Food Guide Pyramid pattern.
2. Color the pyramids' triangles from left to right with the following pattern:
   a. Orange—grains
   b. Green—vegetables
   c. Red—fruits
   d. Yellow—fats and oils
   e. Blue—milk and dairy products
   f. Purple—meat, beans, fish, and nuts
3. Glue one pyramid to construction paper with rubber cement.
4. Cut the other pyramid into sections.
5. Cut small food pictures out of magazines or advertisements and place in a bowl.

continued

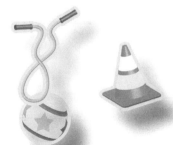

Pyramid Puzzle continued

PROCEDURES:

The child will complete the following steps:

1. Look at the complete Food Guide Pyramid.
2. Take the pieces of his or her pyramid and lay them in order on construction paper.
3. Using glue, glue the pieces to the paper.
4. Select and identify a food from the bowl, with adult assistance if needed.
5. Glue the food in the appropriate color triangle of the Food Guide Pyramid.

NOTE:

Older children may color and cut their own pyramid. Younger children may only have the attention span to complete steps 1–3.

DISCUSSION SUGGESTIONS:

- ✂ People need to eat food from each group to help them grow and stay healthy.
- ✂ Why are some wedges of the pyramid larger than others?
- ✂ The larger wedges mean you can eat more of those foods.
- ✂ What type of food can you eat the most of?
- ✂ What type of food can you eat the least of?

EXPANSIONS:

- ✂ Make a Food Guide Pyramid book by adding pages for each type of food. Cut larger pictures out of magazines and glue on appropriate pages.
- ✂ Visit the web site http://www.mypyramid.gov, which allows you to plug in age, gender, and activity level to see how much food of each group is needed daily.

80

Quick Snack

ADULT PREPARATION:

1. Wash hands.
2. Use paring knife to peel, core, and half apple.
3. Pour 1 cup water and 1–2 tablespoons lemon juice in a bowl.
4. Place the apple in the lemon juice mixture to prevent the apple from turning brown.
5. Put peanut butter and yogurt in separate bowls.
6. Drain liquid from apple halves.
7. Cut banana in half.
8. Put half banana and half apple on plate.

PROCEDURES:

The child will complete the following steps:

1. Wash hands.
2. Peel the banana and cut into pieces.
3. Cut the apple into smaller pieces.
4. Put a spoonful of yogurt and a spoonful of peanut butter in a bowl.
5. Stir the yogurt and peanut butter well.
6. Dip the apple and banana pieces in the yogurt/peanut butter mixture to eat.

DISCUSSION SUGGESTIONS:

- ✄ Sometimes when we are hungry, we have a quick snack that is not healthy.
- ✄ What are some healthy snacks that you can eat?
- ✄ What are some healthy snacks that can be made quickly?

⚠ SAFETY PRECAUTION:

If a child is allergic to peanut butter, omit this ingredient. If a child is lactose intolerant, omit the yogurt and melt the peanut butter in the microwave for approximately 20–30 seconds to produce a thinner consistency for dipping.

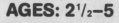

AGES: 2½–5

GROUP SIZE:
4–10 children

DEVELOPMENTAL GOALS:
- ✄ To promote healthy habits
- ✄ To enjoy nutritious food

LEARNING OBJECTIVE:
Using a small banana, a small apple, peanut butter, vanilla, yogurt, a bowl, table knife, and plate, the child will create a quick snack.

MATERIALS:
Paring knife
Apple
Measuring cup
Water
Measuring spoons
Lemon juice
Bowls
Spoons
Peanut butter
Yogurt
Banana
Table knife
Plate

Raisins

AGES: 2½–5

GROUP SIZE:
4–6 children

DEVELOPMENTAL GOALS:
- ✂ To promote nutrition
- ✂ To identify similarities and differences

LEARNING OBJECTIVE:
Using golden and black raisins, the child will sort and determine similarities and differences.

MATERIALS:
Golden raisins
Black raisins
Small cups
Small plates

ADULT PREPARATION:
1. Wash hands.
2. Place a mixture of black and golden raisins in a small cup for each child.
3. Set the raisins and plates on the table.

PROCEDURES:
The child will complete the following steps:
1. Wash hands.
2. Sort the black and the golden raisins onto their plate in two separate groups.
3. Taste the black raisins and then taste the golden raisins.
4. Answer the questions, "How are the raisins the same?" and "How are the raisins different?"

DISCUSSION SUGGESTIONS:
- ✂ Raisins are rich in minerals. [They contain 5% calcium, 8% magnesium, 10% iron and phosphorus, 14% manganese, 15% copper, and 31% potassium (http://elook.org/).]
- ✂ Our bodies need minerals to help us stay healthy and strong.
- ✂ Raisins are a dried fruit.
- ✂ One-half cup of a dried fruit is considered to be a cup of fruit.
- ✂ A cup of fruit is the amount a child 2–3 years old may eat daily.
- ✂ A child 4–8 years old may eat 1 – 1½ cups of fruit daily.

⚠ SAFETY PRECAUTION:
When using small food items like raisins, supervise children closely to prevent choking.

Reading Road Signs

ADULT PREPARATION:

1. Copy and cut duplicate road sign patterns.
2. Cut construction paper squares.
3. Use rubber cement to fix road signs on the construction paper.
4. Lay one set of road signs on the table in a row.
5. Put the other set of road signs in a stack, face down.

PROCEDURES:

The child will complete the following steps:

1. Identify the road signs from left to right, with adult assistance if needed.
2. Discuss with adult how each road sign promotes safety.
3. Select one road sign from the stack.
4. Identify the road sign and place it on top of the identical one in the row.
5. Repeat steps 2–3 until all road signs are matched.

continued

R

AGES: 2½–5

GROUP SIZE:

2–3 children

DEVELOPMENTAL GOALS:

- ✂ To identify common objects
- ✂ To discriminate between likenesses and differences

LEARNING OBJECTIVE:

Using road signs, the child will identify and match the symbols.

MATERIALS:

Road sign patterns (Appendix A24–A29):
Stop sign (Appendix A24)
Railroad crossing (Appendix A25)
Bike trail (Appendix A26)
Walk signal (Appendix A27)
Don't walk signal (Appendix A28)
Yield sign (Appendix A29)
Copy paper
Construction paper
Scissors
Rubber cement

Reading Road Signs continued

DISCUSSION SUGGESTIONS:

✀ Why is it important to know what road signs say?

✀ Knowing what road signs say can keep us safe.

✀ Look at each road sign. How does each sign help keep people safe?

Red Light, Green Light

ADULT PREPARATION:

1. Trace the circular end of the paddle onto red and green construction paper.
2. Cut the circles out.
3. Label the green circle "GO" and the red circle "STOP."
4. Hot glue one circle to each side of the paddle.

PROCEDURES:

The children will complete the following steps:

1. Line up at one end of the playground or yard.
2. Look at the adult holding the red light/green light paddle approximately 30 feet away.
3. When the adult shows the green side of the paddle and says, "Green Light," race towards the adult.
4. When the adult shows the red side of the paddle and says, "Red Light," stop.
5. If forward movement continues during "Red Light," they will return to the starting point.
6. Steps 2–5 are continued until someone reaches the adult.
7. The first child to reach the adult takes a turn to hold the red light/green light paddle and give directions.
8. Repeat steps 1–7.

NOTE:

Avoid saying, "Go!" for the green light. Children will typically run when they hear this word and have difficulty stopping. It may take young children several sessions of playing this game to master the tactic of stopping on command.

DISCUSSION SUGGESTIONS:

✄ Where do you see traffic lights?
✄ How do traffic lights keep us safe?

AGES: 3–5

GROUP SIZE:

6–15 children

DEVELOPMENTAL GOALS:

✄ To stimulate large muscle development
✄ To follow directions

LEARNING OBJECTIVE:

Using a red light/green light paddle, the children will play a game.

MATERIALS:

Paddle (ping pong or paddle ball)
Red and green construction paper
Marker
Scissors
Hot glue gun and glue sticks

Rest and Relaxation

AGES: 3–5

GROUP SIZE:

4–20 children

DEVELOPMENTAL GOALS:

- ✀ To promote a relaxation technique
- ✀ To encourage emotional development

LEARNING OBJECTIVE:

Using a child-size chair and bath towel, the child will achieve a state of rest.

MATERIALS:

Child-size chair
Bath towel

ADULT PREPARATION:

1. Lay a towel on the floor, lengthwise in front of a child-size chair.

PROCEDURES:

The child will complete the following steps:

1. Lay down on the towel on his or her back.
2. Lift legs up onto the chair. Legs should be bent at the knee in a 90° angle.
3. Place arms out straight from the body.
4. Close eyes and do not talk.
5. Hold position the number of minutes equal to his or her age (i.e., a three-year-old would hold the position 3 minutes).
6. If attention span allows, rest in this position longer.

NOTE:

If desired, soft instrumental music may be played in the background. Avoid music with words that might tempt the child to sing along.

DISCUSSION SUGGESTIONS:

- ✀ When a person is rested, they are able to think better.
- ✀ Being rested helps a person stay healthy.

Sack Lunch

ADULT PREPARATION:

1. Remove pages from magazines that contain pictures of food.
2. Write each child's name on an individual lunch sack.

PROCEDURES:

The child will complete the following steps:

1. Discuss healthy versus unhealthy food with adult.
2. Select the lunch bag with his or her name.
3. Look at the pictures of food; cut out the pictures of healthy food and place them in the bag.
4. Identify the foods with sugar and leave them on the table.

DISCUSSION SUGGESTIONS:

✂ It is important to eat foods that are good for us.
✂ Healthy foods help our bodies grow.
✂ Eating too much food with sugar is not good for our bodies.

AGES: 2½–5

GROUP SIZE:
2–4 children

DEVELOPMENTAL GOALS:

✂ To promote fine motor skills
✂ To recognize nutritious food

LEARNING OBJECTIVE:

Using a lunch-size paper bag, magazine pictures of food, and child-size scissors, the child will identify healthy food.

MATERIALS:

Magazines with pictures of food
Marker
Lunch-size paper bag
Child-size scissors

S

Seatbelt Safety

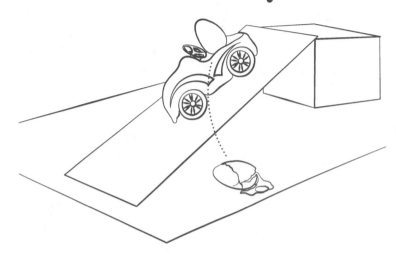

GROUP SIZE:

3–6 children

DEVELOPMENTAL GOALS:

✂ To develop knowledge of seat belt safety

✂ To coordinate muscles

LEARNING OBJECTIVE:

Using eggs, toy cars or trucks, masking tape, and inclines, the child will demonstrate the importance of wearing seat belts.

MATERIALS:

Newspapers
Plastic tarp (optional)
Wooden blocks
Wooden planks
Eggs
Two toy cars or trucks (large enough to loosely hold an egg)
Masking tape

ADULT PREPARATION:

1. Place newspapers on the floor. If the floor is carpeted, place a plastic tarp under the newspaper or conduct the activity outside.
2. Place blocks in two stacks.
3. Place a wooden plank against each stack, creating two inclines.
4. Set a raw egg in each vehicle.
5. Tape one egg to one of the vehicles. Leave the other egg untaped.

PROCEDURES:

The child will complete the following steps:

1. Listen to the adult explain, "It is important to wear seat belts or sit in a car seat in the car. The tape is like a seat belt. What will happen to the egg that is not strapped into the car?"
2. Place the vehicles at the top of the inclines.
3. Let the cars travel down the inclines.

NOTES:

The egg not taped into the car should break upon impact. The taped egg should remain intact. Eggs may be boiled to reduce clean-up. Wash hands after touching eggs.

continued

Seatbelt Safety continued

DISCUSSION SUGGESTIONS:

- ✀ It is important to wear a seatbelt or sit in a car seat to keep us safe.
- ✀ Everyone in the vehicle needs to either wear a seatbelt or sit in a car seat.
- ✀ Seat belts need to be worn properly to work.

Stop, Drop, and Roll

Stop, Drop and Roll

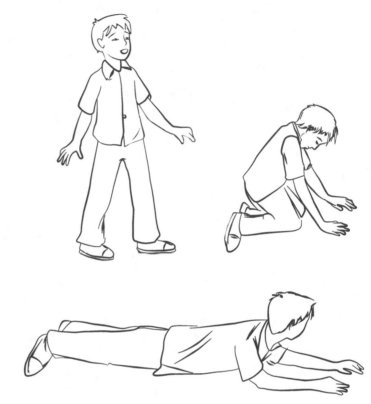

Stop, Drop and Roll

AGES: 3–5

GROUP SIZE:

4–6 children

DEVELOPMENTAL GOALS:

✂ To promote self-help skills

✂ To role-play life situations

LEARNING OBJECTIVE:

Using the chant "Stop, drop and roll," the child will practice fire safety.

MATERIALS:

Paper
Marker
Masking tape
Book: *Stop Drop and Roll* by Margery Cuyler

ADULT PREPARATION:

1. Write *Stop, drop, and roll* in large font on paper.

2. Fix the paper to the wall at the children's eye level with masking tape or other approved adhesive.

PROCEDURES:

The child will complete the following steps:

1. Listen to the adult read *Stop Drop and Roll* by Margery Cuyler.

2. Explain why a person would stop, drop, and roll, to reinforce what was heard in the story.

3. Practice the "stop, drop, and roll" procedure.

continued

90

Stop, Drop, and Roll continued

DISCUSSION SUGGESTIONS:

- ✄ Practice "stop, drop, and roll" at home.
- ✄ "Stop, drop, and roll" is used to keep people safe when they are involved in a fire.
- ✄ Before you "stop, drop, and roll" you must move away from the dangerous situation.

BOOK SUGGESTION:

Stop Drop and Roll by Margery Cuyler. (New York: Simon & Schuster Books for Young Readers, 2001). Jessica worries about fire safety until she becomes knowledgeable about the rules. She even demonstrates "stop, drop and roll" for a school assembly.

Sunscreen, Safety Screen

AGES: 2¹/₂–5

GROUP SIZE:

6–12 children

DEVELOPMENTAL GOALS:

✂ To develop vocabulary

✂ To promote healthy practices

LEARNING OBJECTIVE:

Using the song board, towels, and empty bottles of sunscreen, the children will sing *Sunscreen, Safety Screen.*

MATERIALS:

Poster board
Marker
Magazine pictures or advertisements of sunscreen
Scissors
Rubber cement
Empty bottles of sunscreen (one for each child)
Scissors
Marker
Rubber cement
Water
Towels (one for each child)

ADULT PREPARATION:

1. Write words to *Sunscreen, Safety Screen* on the poster board.
2. Cut pictures of sunscreen out of magazines or advertisements.
3. Use rubber cement to glue pictures of sunscreen to the poster.
4. Rinse all sunscreen out of bottles with water. Let dry.
5. Set out one towel for each child in a semicircle or circle.
6. Place an empty bottle of sunscreen on each towel.

PROCEDURES:

The child will complete the following steps:

1. Sit down on a towel with an empty bottle of sunscreen.
2. Pretend to put sunscreen on while singing the following song to the tune of *Row, Row, Row Your Boat.*

> *Sunscreen, Safety Screen*
> Sunscreen is good for you.
> We put it on to play.
> It's a safety screen from sun,
> to keep our skin this way.

NOTE:

Depending upon the severity, sunburns may be classified as a first- or second-degree burn. After exposure to the sun, a burn may take 3 to 12 hours to become evident (Herr, 2004).

DISCUSSION SUGGESTIONS:

✂ When should people wear sunscreen?
✂ Why do people wear sunscreen?
✂ Sunscreen helps keep our skin healthy.

Taste

ADULT PREPARATION:

1. Copy the pattern of the tongue.
2. Label the parts of the tongue by taste.
   a. Front of the tongue—salty and sweet
   b. Sides of the tongue—sour
   c. Back of the tongue—bitter
3. Wash hands.
4. Cut small pieces of sour pickle and place them on a plate.
5. Pour a very small amount of decaffeinated coffee in small individual cups.
6. Put the following food on individual plates for each child: piece of pickle, spoonful of honey, and one potato chip.

PROCEDURES:

The child will complete the following steps:

1. Wash hands.
2. Listen to the adult explain that the tongue has taste buds to taste four different kinds of food: sweet, salty, sour, or bitter.

continued

93

Taste continued

3. Using a spoon, taste the honey.

4. Answer the adult's question, "How does it taste, sour, sweet, salty, or bitter?"

5. Use a yellow marker to dot a taste bud on the front of the tongue.

6. Eat the potato chip.

7. Answer the adult's question, "How does it taste, sour, sweet, salty, or bitter?"

8. Use a brown marker to dot a taste bud on the front of the tongue.

9. Taste the pickle.

10. Answer the adult's question, "How does it taste, sour, sweet, salty, or bitter?"

11. Use the green marker to dot a taste bud on the side of the tongue.

12. Sip the decaffeinated coffee.

13. Answer the adult's question, "How does it taste, sour, sweet, salty, or bitter?"

14. Dot a taste bud on the back of the tongue with a black marker.

DISCUSSION SUGGESTIONS:

- ✂ We use our tongue to taste.
- ✂ Foods have different tastes.
- ✂ Some things taste sweet, sour, salty, or bitter.

⚠ SAFETY PRECAUTION:

Before conducting this activity, check for food allergies. If a child has a food sensitivity, substitute a similar tasting food.

BOOK SUGGESTION:

Tasting by Sharon Gordon (New York: Children's Press, 2001). This book is part of the Rookie Read-About Health books. It has an illustration of the tongue and photographs of children tasting various foods.

94

Telephone Numbers

AGES: 2¹/₂–5

GROUP SIZE:

1 child

DEVELOPMENTAL GOALS:

✄ To promote self-help skills

✄ To identify numbers

LEARNING OBJECTIVE:

Using rhythm sticks and a telephone, the child will practice reciting their phone number.

MATERIALS:

Telephone card pattern (Appendix B9)
Copy paper
Marker
Telephone
Rhythm sticks

ADULT PREPARATION:

1. Make a copy of the telephone card pattern.
2. Write the child's name and telephone number on the card. Include the area code.

PROCEDURES:

The child will complete the following steps:

1. Listen to the adult say, "It is important for you to know your phone number when you need to call home or in an emergency."
2. Identify the numbers on the telephone card.
3. Say the numbers hitting the rhythm sticks together each time a number is said.
4. Repeat the numbers in a chant fashion while hitting the rhythm sticks.
5. Go over step 3 until comfortable with the sequence of numbers.
6. Dial or push numbers on the telephone while repeating the number chant.

continued

Telephone Numbers continued

NOTE:

Many areas do not need to dial an area code to reach a local number. However, it is required in metropolitan areas and when making out-of-state calls.

DISCUSSION SUGGESTIONS:

- ✂ Why is it important to know your telephone number?
- ✂ Knowing our telephone numbers can help keep us safe.
- ✂ If we know our telephone number, we can call home when we need to.

Time for Tea Testing

ADULT PREPARATION:

1. Make a copy of the teapot pattern.
2. Wash hands.
3. Heat water in a pan or tea kettle.
4. Divide water between two pitchers.
5. Add a different type of green teabag to each pitcher.
6. Allow the tea to step for 5 minutes.
7. Remove the teabags and let the tea cool to a lukewarm temperature.
8. Cover the table with a tablecloth.
9. Put tea into two separate child-size pitchers.
10. Place a different color of sticker on each pitcher.
11. Place a matching sticker on the teapots on the chart.
12. Set cups, saucers, and napkins on the table.

PROCEDURES:

The children will complete the following steps:

1. Wash hands.
2. Put a napkin in his or her lap as they listen to the adult explain, "It is good manners to put your napkin in your lap, in case you spill."
3. Take turns pouring a small amount of one tea into each other's cup.
4. Sip the tea.
5. Blot the mouth with the napkin. Return the napkin to the lap.
6. When finished with the first cup, pour a small amount of the second tea into cups.
7. Repeat steps 3–4.
8. Discuss which tea he or she prefers with tablemates.
9. Identify the color of sticker on the pitcher with tea they prefer.
10. Select a sticker matching that color and put it on the tea chart. Put the sticker in the column with the teapot with the same color of sticker.
11. Once everyone has sampled the tea, count the number of stickers in each column.

AGES: 2½–5

GROUP SIZE:
2–5 children

DEVELOPMENTAL GOALS:
✄ To enhance social development
✄ To promote fine motor skills

LEARNING OBJECTIVE:
Using two types of decaffeinated tea, napkins, child-size pitchers, cups, and saucers, the children will relax with a warm beverage.

MATERIALS:
Tea chart pattern (Appendix B10)
Copy paper
Water
Pan or tea kettle
Two pitchers
Two different flavors of decaffeinated green tea
Tablecloth
Two child-size pitchers
Two colors of stickers
Child-size plastic teacups and saucers
Napkins

continued

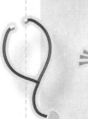

Time for Tea Testing continued

The adult will complete the following steps:

1. Write the number of stickers present in each column.
2. Ask the children, "Which tea did most people like?" and "Which tea did people like the least?"

DISCUSSION SUGGESTIONS:

- ✄ Decaffeinated green tea may help a person relax.
- ✄ It also acts as an antioxidant.
- ✄ Antioxidants help protect the body.

BOOK SUGGESTION:

Tea for Me, Tea for You by Laura Rader. (New York: HarperCollins, 2003). The tea party quickly goes from 1 to 10 as a little pig keeps expanding the number in her party.

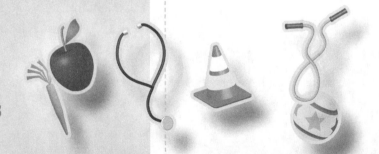

Underground and Above-Ground Vegetables

ABOVE-GROUND

UNDERGROUND

ADULT PREPARATION:

1. Copy, color, cut, and glue a picture of the carrots, potato, radish, yams, broccoli, corn, peas, and pumpkin on squares of construction paper.

2. Copy and color the picture of the garden.

3. Cover the vegetables and the garden with clear contact paper, or laminate them.

continued

AGES: 3–5

GROUP SIZE:
4–8 children

DEVELOPMENTAL GOALS:
- ✂ To develop classification skills
- ✂ To promote social development

LEARNING OBJECTIVE:
Using pictures of vegetables and a garden, the children will take turns identifying and classifying vegetables.

MATERIALS:
Patterns of plants (Appendix A31–A39):
Carrots (Appendix A31)
Potato (Appendix A32)
Radish (Appendix A33)
Yams (Appendix A34)
Broccoli (Appendix A35)
Corn (Appendix A36)
Peas (Appendix A37)

99

Underground and Above-Ground Vegetables continued

MATERIALS:

Pumpkin
(Appendix A38)
Pattern of a view
of the top and
underneath a garden
(Appendix 39)
Markers
Colored pencils or
crayons
Construction paper
Scissors
Rubber cement
Clear contact paper or
laminator
Hook and loop tape
Basket
Masking tape

4. Fix hook and loop tape to the back of the vegetables.

5. Fix four squares of hook and loop tape above and below the soil level of the garden. The distance between hook and loop squares should equal the size of the vegetable squares.

6. Put the pictures of the vegetables into a basket.

7. Put the garden on the wall with masking tape.

PROCEDURES:

The children will complete the following steps:

1. Sit in a circle or semicircle.

2. Listen to adult explain, "Some vegetables grow on top of the ground where we can see them. Other vegetables grow underneath the ground. The only thing we see is their leaves on top of the ground."

3. Take turns selecting a vegetable from the basket.

4. Identify the vegetable.

5. Determine if it grows underground or above-ground, with adult assistance if necessary.

6. Fix the vegetable to the hook and loop tape on the garden, either placing it underground or above-ground, depending on where it grows.

7. Take turns repeating steps 3–6.

DISCUSSION SUGGESTIONS:

✂ Vegetables are a healthy food.

✂ Vegetables help us grow and help the body fight infections.

✂ Always wash vegetables before eating or cooking them.

✂ Many vegetables may be eaten raw or cooked.

EXPANSION:

Place the vegetables and garden in the math center and allow smaller groups or individual children to continue the activity.

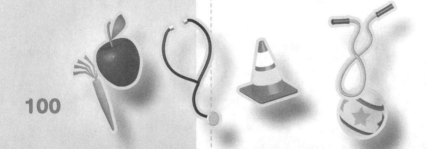

100

Using "No"

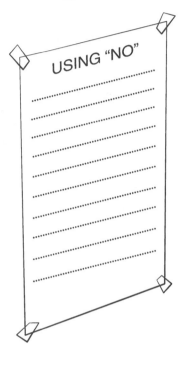

USING "NO"

AGES: 2½–5

GROUP SIZE:
4–12 children

DEVELOPMENTAL GOALS:
- ✄ To promote safety
- ✄ To participate in a group

LEARNING OBJECTIVE:
Using the song *Using "No,"* the children will integrate safety responses.

MATERIALS:
Poster board
Markers
Masking tape

ADULT PREPARATION:

1. Write the words to *Using "No"* on poster board.
2. Hang the song poster at the children's eye level with masking tape or other approved material.

PROCEDURES:

The children will complete the following steps:

1. Sit in a circle or semicircle.
2. Listen to the adult explain, "We should never go with strangers."
3. Sing the following song to the tune of *If You're Happy and You Know It.*

continued

Using "No" continued

Using "No"
If a stranger comes to you,
To find their dog,
Say, "NO!"
If a stranger comes to you
To find their dog,
Say, "NO!"
If a stranger comes to you
And wants you to go with them,
If a stranger comes to you,
Say, "NO!"

If a stranger comes to you,
To take you home,
Say, "NO!"
If a stranger comes to you,
To take you home,
Say, "NO!"
If a stranger comes to you
And says your mom sent me,
If a stranger comes to you,
Say, "NO!"

If a stranger comes to you,
And says she's lost,
Say, "NO!"
If a stranger comes to you,
And says she's lost,
Say, "NO!"

If a stranger comes to you,
And wants you to show her the way,
If a stranger comes to you,
Say, "NO!"

continued

Using "No" continued

If a stranger comes to you,
Say, "NO!" and run.
If a stranger comes to you,
Say, "NO!" and run.
If a stranger comes to you,
Then you know what to do,
If a stranger comes to you,
Say, "NO!" and run.

DISCUSSION SUGGESTIONS:

✂ Knowing when to say "no" helps keep children safe.

✂ Most strangers may be nice people, but some of them are not nice.

✂ Because some are not nice, it is important to stay away from strangers. Do not speak with them.

V

Vegetable Soup

AGES: 2½–5

GROUP SIZE:
4–10 children

DEVELOPMENTAL GOALS:
- ✂ To promote self-help skills
- ✂ To stimulate social development by taking turns

LEARNING OBJECTIVE:
Using 15-ounce cans of vegetable broth, carrots, green beans, corn, potatoes, spaghetti sauce, a measuring cup, pot, and long-handled wooden spoon, the children will make vegetable soup.

MATERIALS:
15 oz. cans of:
Vegetable broth
Sliced carrots
Cut green beans
Corn
Sliced potatoes
Spaghetti sauce

ADULT PREPARATION:

1. Wash hands.
2. Remove all lids from the cans with a smooth-edge can opener.
3. Measure 1 cup of spaghetti sauce.

PROCEDURES:

The children will complete the following steps:

1. Take turns emptying the cans of vegetables and their liquids into the pot.
2. Pour the cup of spaghetti sauce into the pot.
3. Take turns stirring the ingredients with a long-handled wooden spoon.

The adult will complete the following steps:

1. Put the pot on the stove on medium heat.
2. Periodically stir ingredients as the soup warms.
3. Once warm, remove the soup from heat; ladle the soup into bowls for the children to eat at snack time.

DISCUSSION SUGGESTIONS:

- ✂ Children who are 2–3 years-old need 1 cup of vegetables each day.
- ✂ Children who are 4–8 years-old need 1½ cups of vegetables each day.
- ✂ A cup of raw vegetables equals the cup size of the Food Guide Pyramid.
- ✂ A half cup of cooked vegetables equals a Food Guide Pyramid cup.
- ✂ Vegetable soup is an excellent source of vegetables.

BOOK SUGGESTIONS:

There are many versions of *Stone Soup* that are suitable for preschoolers. *Stone Soup* features travelers who comes to town and want the townspeople to share food with them. The undaunted travelers start a

continued

104

Vegetable Soup continued

soup with a stone, and eventually all contribute various foods to the pot. Versions include:

✄ *Stone Soup* by Heather Forest. (Little Rock, AR: August House LittleFolk, 1998). This version ends with a recipe for stone soup.

✄ *Stone Soup* by Jon J. Muth (New York: Scholastic Press, 2003). Muth's retelling of this classic tale is set in China. The travelers are monks who seek to spread enlightenment.

✄ Another book suggestion that would be appropriate for two-year-olds is *Growing Vegetable Soup* by Lois Ehlert. It has simple text and bright, colorful illustrations that start with planting vegetable seeds and end with eating soup. The inside jacket cover also contains a recipe for vegetable soup.

MATERIALS:

Smooth-edge can
  opener
Measuring cup
Large pot
Long-handled wooden
  spoon
Ladle
Bowls
Spoons

Vitamin Store

AGES: 2½–5

GROUP SIZE:

2–3 children

DEVELOPMENTAL GOALS:

✂ To promote self-help skills

✂ To practice various roles

LEARNING OBJECTIVE:

Using a vitamin chart, cash register, play money, wallet or coin purse, bags, and empty vitamin or prescription bottles, the children will role-play a pharmacist and customer.

MATERIALS:

Marker
Vitamin Chart
    (Appendix B11)
Paper
Sticky labels
Empty vitamin or
    prescription bottles
Copy paper
Cash register
Masking tape
Play money
Wallet or coin purse
Lunch-size bags

ADULT PREPARATION:

1. Write *Vitamin Store* in large font on a sheet of paper

2. Write *Vitamin A, Vitamin B, Vitamin C, Vitamin D, Vitamin E, and Vitamin K* on sticky labels.

3. Put the labels on the empty vitamin or prescription bottles.

4. Copy the vitamin chart.

5. Set the vitamin chart beside the cash register.

6. Hang the sign *Vitamin Store* on the wall with masking tape.

7. Put play money in the cash register and wallet or coin purse.

continued

Vitamin Store continued

PROCEDURES:

The children will complete the following steps:

1. Assign roles of clerk and customer(s).
2. The clerk sits behind the cash register.
3. The customer(s) takes a wallet or coin purse.
4. The clerk greets the customer and asks what type of vitamin they are looking for.
5. Each customer looks at the vitamin chart and decides what he or she wants (e.g., a vitamin to help with eyes).
6. The clerk looks at the vitamin chart and decides which vitamin the customer needs.
7. The clerk selects the correct vitamin, puts it in a bag, and rings up the total on the cash register.
8. Each customer pays for his or her vitamins.
9. Steps 1–8 are repeated with the children switching roles.

DISCUSSION SUGGESTIONS:

✄ Vitamins help keep people healthy.

✄ Most vitamins come from the healthy food we eat.

✄ Many people take vitamins when they don't eat right, or to help them reduce the effects of stress.

Vocal Cord Vibration

AGES: 2¹/₂–5

GROUP SIZE:

4–6 children

DEVELOPMENTAL GOALS:

- ✂ To develop the sense of touch
- ✂ To note differences in sound

LEARNING OBJECTIVE:

Using his or her hand and vocal cords, the child will feel the different vibrations between high and low sounds.

MATERIALS:

None needed

ADULT PREPARATION:

1. Clear an area for group time.

PROCEDURES:

The child will complete the following steps:

1. Hold his or her hand over the front of their neck and hum.
2. Answer the adult's question, "What do you feel?"
3. Listen to the adult say, "That's your vocal cords."

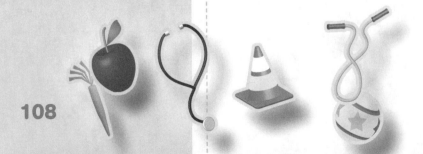

continued

Vocal Cord Vibration continued

4. Make a high sound while holding his or her hand over their vocal cords.

5. Make a low sound while holding his or her hand over their vocal cords.

6. Answer the adult's question, "What is the difference between the vocal cord vibration between the high sound and the low sound?"

NOTE:

The lower pitch should vibrate more than the higher pitch.

DISCUSSION SUGGESTIONS:

✄ It is important to take care of your throat and your vocal cords.

✄ Drink plenty of fluids.

✄ Screaming a lot can strain your vocal cords; try to speak in a normal voice.

Washing Hands

AGES: 2¹/₂–5

GROUP SIZE:

2–4 children

DEVELOPMENTAL GOALS:

✂ To promote self-help skills

✂ To understand the importance of washing hands

LEARNING OBJECTIVE:

Using florescent paint, soap, water, and a black light, the children will wash their hands.

MATERIALS:

Markers
Small poster board
Laminator and laminating film
Masking tape
Florescent paint
Liquid hand soap
Water
Paper towels
Black light

ADULT PREPARATION:

1. Using markers write the words to the *Hand Washing Song* on the small poster board.
2. Laminate the song board and fix it to the wall above the sink where the children wash their hands.

PROCEDURES:

The children will complete the following steps:

1. Listen to the adult explain, "We wash our hands, to wash off germs. Washing our hands keeps us healthy."
2. Rub a pea-sized amount of florescent paint onto hands.
3. Sing the *Hand Washing Song,* while washing hands with liquid soap and water.

Hand Washing Song (sung to the tune of *Mary Had a Little Lamb*)

I will wash my hands with soap,

Hands with soap,

Hands with soap.

I will wash my hands with soap 'til germs go down the drain.

I will rinse my hands with water,

Hands with water,

Hands with water.

I will wash my hands with water 'til germs go down the drain.

3. Dry hands with a paper towel and dispose of the towel in the trash.
4. Look at hands under the black light.
5. If florescent paint is visible under the black light, repeat steps 2–4.

Yellow Jacket Safety

ADULT PREPARATION:

1. Create antennae headbands for children by wrapping one end of the pipe cleaner around the headband. Put two pipe cleaners on each headband.
2. Stand the pipe cleaners at a 90° angle from the headband.
3. Stick a foam ball on each end of the pipe cleaners.
4. Write the words to *Yellow Jacket Freeze* on the poster board.
5. Display the song board in the group time area.

PROCEDURES:

The children will complete the following steps:

1. Listen to the adult explain, "Yellow jackets are bees. When they fly around us, we need to stand still so they will fly away."
2. Half of the children will put on headbands. They are the bees.
3. The children will sing the following song:

Yellow Jacket Freeze

When yellow jackets come buzzing around,   (*Bees buzz around.*)
C•F•F•C•C•C•F•F•F•C

Root your feet right to the ground,
G•G•D•D•G•G•D

Do the yellow jacket freeze.
D•D•C•C•D•E•F   (*Children without headbands stand still, bees still buzz around.*)

The bees won't bother us on the hill,   (*Bees buzz around.*)
C•F•F•C•C•C•F•F•F•C

If we all stand so very still,
G•G•D•D•G•G•D

Do the yellow jacket freeze.
C•F•F•C•C•C•F•F•F•C   (*Children without headbands stand still, bees still buzz around.*)

AGES: 2½–5

GROUP SIZE:

4–8 children

DEVELOPMENTAL GOALS:

✂ To promote safe practices

✂ To respect insects

LEARNING OBJECTIVE:

Using a song board and antennae headbands, children will participate in a safety song about yellow jackets.

MATERIALS:

Headbands
12" pipe cleaners
Foam balls
Markers
Poster board

continued

Yellow Jacket Safety continued

Yellow jackets don't want us near,

C•F•F•C•C•C•F•F•F•C

(Bees buzz away from other children.)

So keep your distance without fear,

G•G•D•D•D•G•G•D

Do the yellow jacket freeze.

C•F•F•C•C•C•F•F•F•C

(Children without headbands stand still.)

4. Children will take turns being bees and sing the song again.

NOTE:

Musical notes given refer to middle C on the piano or keyboard. Each note corresponds to one syllable.

DISCUSSION SUGGESTIONS:

✂ To stay healthy, it is important to be calm when around bees.

✂ Bees will usually leave a person alone when the person is still and quiet.

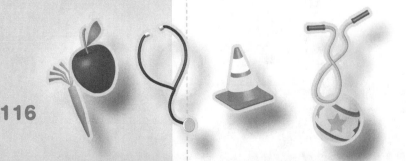

Yoga

AGES: 4–5

GROUP SIZE:
4–6 children

DEVELOPMENTAL GOALS:
- ✂ To promote relaxation
- ✂ To develop large muscles

LEARNING OBJECTIVE:
Following the adult's directions, the children will participate in yoga moves.

MATERIALS:
None needed

ADULT PREPARATION:

1. Clear an area for children to be able to move without touching.

PROCEDURES:

The children will complete the following steps:

1. To create the mountain pose:
   a. Stand up straight with feet together, flat on the floor.
   b. Hang arms to the side, with fingers pointing straight to the ground.
   c. Relax the shoulders.
   d. Close eyes, breathe deeply, inhale and exhale.
   e. Count each time he or she inhales. At first simply count to 10.
2. To create the triangle pose:
   a. Stand with the feet apart.
   b. Lift arms until they are parallel to the floor.

continued

Yoga continued

    c. Turn right foot so the heel faces the other foot.

    d. Blow air out through the mouth and bend over at the waist until right hand touches right foot.

    e. Inhale as left arm is held straight in the air.

    f. Turn head and look up at left hand.

    g. Exhale as left arm is lowered.

    h. Inhale while resuming standing position.

    i. Repeat steps with the left side.

DISCUSSION SUGGESTIONS:

- Yoga is a healthy form of exercise.
- Yoga helps aid in relaxation and digestion.

BOOK SUGGESTIONS:

- *Children's Book of Yoga* by Thia Luby (Sante Fe, NM: Clear Light Publishers, 1998) gives the rationale for children doing yoga. It is laid out with photographs and directions for doing the simplest movements first and then progresses to the more difficult. It also gives poses to relieve common childhood ailments and poses to work on specific areas of the body.

- To participate in other yoga postures, read *My Daddy is a Pretzel* by Baron Baptiste. (Cambridge, MA: Barefoot Books, 2004). This book contains colorful illustrations of adults and children participating in yoga. Step-by-step directions are given.

118

Yogurt Tasting

AGES: 2½–5

GROUP SIZE:
4–12 children

DEVELOPMENTAL GOALS:
- ✄ To ingest adequate amounts of calcium into the diet
- ✄ To develop number skills

LEARNING OBJECTIVE:
Using different types of yogurt and a graph, the child will determine the group's favorite yogurt.

MATERIALS:
Poster board
Markers
Yardstick
Adult scissors
Four different flavors of yogurt
Tablespoons
Paper plates
Spoons
Glue stick
Hot glue gun (optional)

ADULT PREPARATION:

1. Write *Yogurt* at the top of the poster board.
2. Divide the poster board into four columns.
3. At the bottom of each column, write one of the four flavors of yogurt.
4. A lid from each type of yogurt may also be glued on the bottom of the column.
5. Cut circles from construction paper that corresponds to the flavors of yogurt (i.e., red for strawberry, blue for blueberry, white for vanilla, orange for peach).
6. Wash hands.
7. Place a tablespoon of each yogurt on each quadrant of the child's plate.

PROCEDURES:

The child will complete the following steps:

1. Wash hands.
2. Taste each type of yogurt.

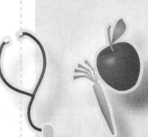

continued

Yogurt Tasting continued

3. Decide which yogurt he or she like best.

4. Select the color of circle that corresponds to the type of yogurt the child likes.

5. Using the glue stick, paste the circle in the corresponding column on the poster board.

6. When all children have sampled the yogurt, count how many circles are in each column.

7. Answer the questions, "Which column has more circles?" and "Which yogurt does the class like best?"

DISCUSSION SUGGESTIONS:

✄ Yogurt is an excellent source of calcium.

✄ Calcium is needed to build strong bones and teeth.

✄ Children two- to eight-years-old should have 2 cups of calcium-rich food or milk each day.

SAFETY PRECAUTION:

If a child is allergic to dairy products, ask the parent to bring in soy yogurt.

Zinc Oxide

AGES: 3–5

GROUP SIZE:

3–6 children

DEVELOPMENTAL GOALS:

✂ To practice inferring

✂ To demonstrate fine motor control

LEARNING OBJECTIVE:

Using zinc ointment, a cotton swab, an egg, and colored water, the child will demonstrate how a water-resistant material promotes good health.

MATERIALS:

Pan
Water
Eggs (one for each child)
Spoons
Zinc oxide
Small bowls
Hot water
Food coloring
Tablespoon
White vinegar
Clear cups
Permanent marker
Smock
Cotton swab
Paper towels

ADULT PREPARATION:

1. Using the pan, place one egg per child in water.
2. Bring eggs to a boil. Continue boiling for 3 minutes.
3. Drain the water off the eggs.
4. Allow the eggs to cool.
5. Put zinc ointment in a bowl.
6. Mix hot water, food coloring, and a tablespoon of vinegar in clear cups. Use a separate cup for each color used.
7. Use a permanent marker to write child's name on the bottom of the egg.
8. Wash hands.

PROCEDURES:

The child will complete the following steps:

1. Put on a smock.
2. Use a cotton swab to decorate the egg with zinc ointment.

continued

Zinc Oxide continued

3. Place the egg in the colored water.
4. While the egg is resting in the color, listen to the adult say, "Zinc ointment protects our skin from sunburn or from getting wet when we have a rash. Babies use it for diaper rash. What do you think will happen to the spots of the egg with zinc ointment?"
5. With adult help, the child will remove the egg from the colored water with a spoon.
6. Gently dry the egg and rub the ointment off the egg with a paper towel.
7. Wash hands.

NOTE:

The spots covered with zinc oxide will not color. Use an ointment like Desitin® for this activity. It is made up of 40% zinc oxide; most other diaper ointments contain only 10–16%.

DISCUSSION SUGGESTIONS:

✂ Zinc Oxide is used to keep skin healthy.

✂ It can help keep a baby's bottom dry when they have a diaper rash.

✂ It can also help people keep from getting sunburn when a small area keeps getting burnt.

✂ Noses get sunburned very easily. Some people protect their sunburned nose by putting Zinc Oxide on.

SAFETY PRECAUTION:

Always wash hands after handling eggs.

Zucchini

ADULT PREPARATION:

1. Preheat the oven to 350°.
2. Wash hands.
3. Wash, peel, and cut the ends off the zucchini.
4. Grate the zucchini.
5. Place zucchini, olive oil, egg substitute, self-rising flour, and shredded cheese in separate bowls.
6. Optional: Place the salt in a bowl.
7. Remove paper liner from the foil muffin liner.
8. Write each child's name on the bottom of the foil muffin liner with the permanent marker.

PROCEDURES:

The child will complete the following steps:

1. Wash hands.
2. Select the muffin liner with his or her name.
3. Measure and place the following ingredients in a bowl, mixing them well:
   a. 2 tablespoons and 2 teaspoons of zucchini
   b. 1 teaspoon of olive oil
   c. 1 tablespoon and 1 teaspoon of egg substitute
   d. 2 teaspoons of self-rising flour
   e. 1 tablespoon and 1 teaspoon of shredded cheese
   f. Optional: Pinch of salt
4. Spoon the mixture into the foil muffin liner, with adult assistance if needed.

The adult will complete the following steps:

1. Place the liner on the baking sheet.
2. When the baking sheet is full, bake the zucchini for 30–35 minutes.

AGES: 2–5

GROUP SIZE:
4–6 children

DEVELOPMENTAL GOALS:

- To develop nutritious habits
- To practice measuring

LEARNING OBJECTIVE:

Using zucchini, olive oil, egg substitute, self-rising flour, cheese, and cooking utensils, the child will make a nutritious snack.

MATERIALS:

Zucchini
Vegetable peeler
Paring knife
Cutting board
Grater
Olive oil
Egg Substitute
Self-rising flour
Shredded cheese
Bowls
Salt (optional)
Jumbo foil muffin liners
Permanent marker
Measuring spoons
Spoons
Baking sheet

continued

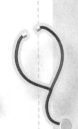

Zucchini continued

DISCUSSION SUGGESTIONS:

- ✂ Zucchini is a healthy vegetable.
- ✂ Zucchini is a good source of Vitamin C.
- ✂ Vitamin C helps a person keep from getting sick.
- ✂ Zucchini can grow very large, but the smaller zucchini have more flavor.

References and Activities Book List

Baptiste, B. (2004). *My daddy is a pretzel: Yoga for parents and kids.* Cambridge, MA: Barefoot Books.

Cuyler, M. (2001). *Stop drop and roll.* New York: Simon and Schuster Books for Young Readers.

Dacey, J. S., & Fiore, L. B. (2000). *Your anxious child.* San Francisco, CA: Jossey-Bass.

Ehlert, L. (1987). *Growing vegetable soup.* San Diego, CA: Harcourt Brace & Company.

Ehrlich, F. (2003). *Does a tiger open wide?* New York: Blue Apple Books.

Forest, H. (1998). *Stone soup.* Little Rock, AR: August House Littlefolk.

Herr, J. (2004). *Working with young children.* Tinley Park, Illinois: Goodheart-Willcox Company, Inc.

Hise, P. (2004, April). Orange alert: Protect yourself from foodborne illness. *Vegetarian Times, 320,* 79–83.

Hughes, M. (2004). *First visit to the dentist.* Chicago: Raintree.

Landau, E. (1999). *Bananas.* New York: Children's Press.

Luby, T. (1998). *Children's book of yoga.* Santa Fe, NM: Clear Light Publishers.

Moss, G. (1970). *Arthur's artichoke.* New York: Dial Press.

Muth, J. J. (2003). *Stone soup.* New York: Scholastic Press.

Raatma, L. (1999). *Safety at the swimming pool.* Mankato, MN: Bridgestone Books.

Rand, G. (2002). *Little flower.* New York: Henry Holt and Company.

Risk, M. (1996). *I want my banana!* New York: Barron's Educational Series, Inc.

Tarpley, N. A. (1998). *I love my hair!* Boston: Little, Brown and Company.

Wells, R. (1973) *Noisy Nora.* New York: Dial Books for Young Readers.

Zonka, P. (2003) *Jessica's x-ray.* Toronto, Ontario: Firefly Books.

Zuravicky, O. (2004). *The galloping book.* New York: The Rosen Publishing Group, Inc.

Appendix A

A1. APPLE

APRICOT

ARTICHOKE

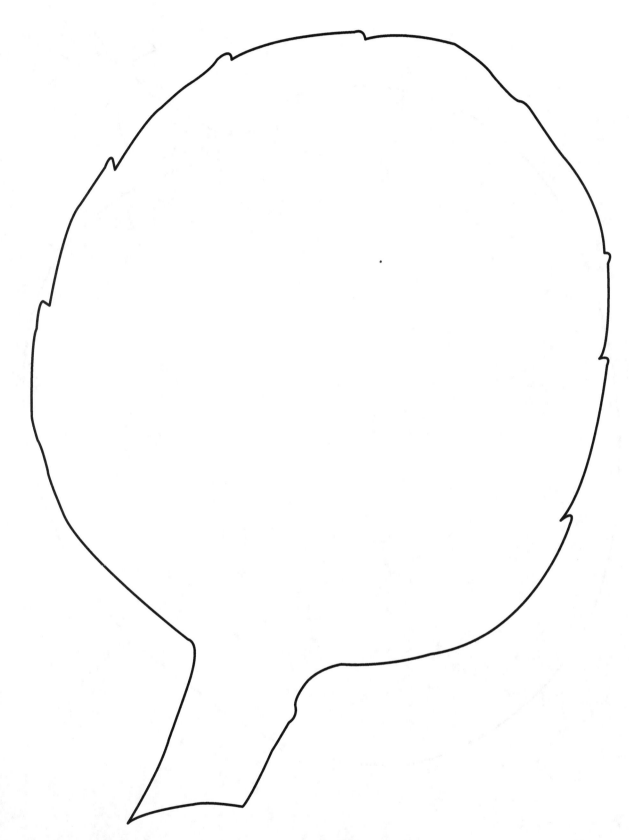

A2. STAIRS WITH SAFETY GATE OPEN

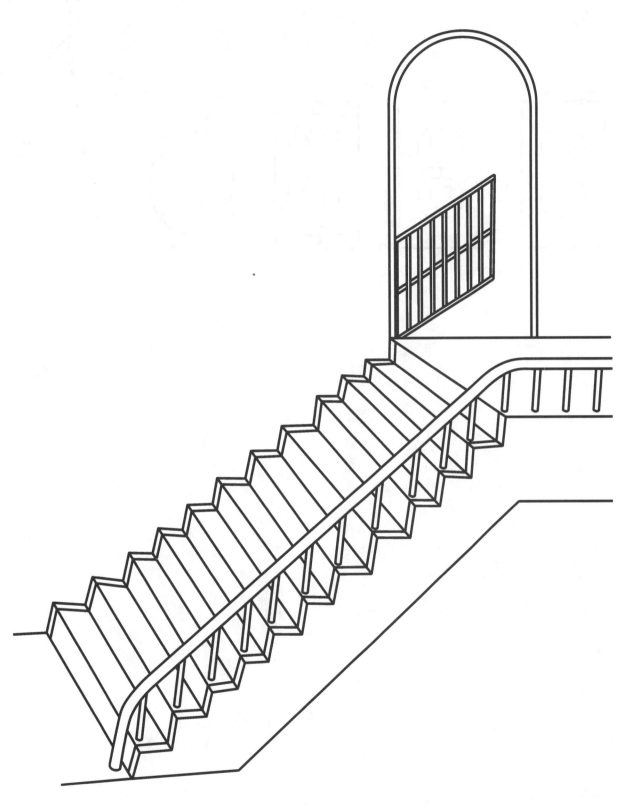

A3. ELECTRICAL OUTLET WITH COVERS BESIDE IT ON FLOOR

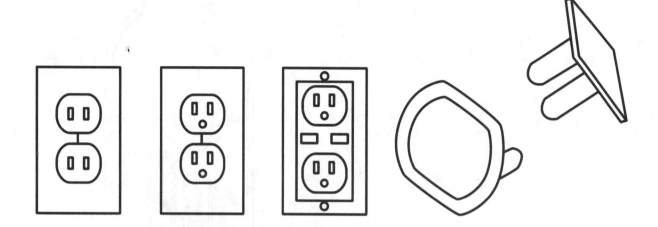

A4. ELECTRICAL CORD DRAPED ACROSS THE FLOOR

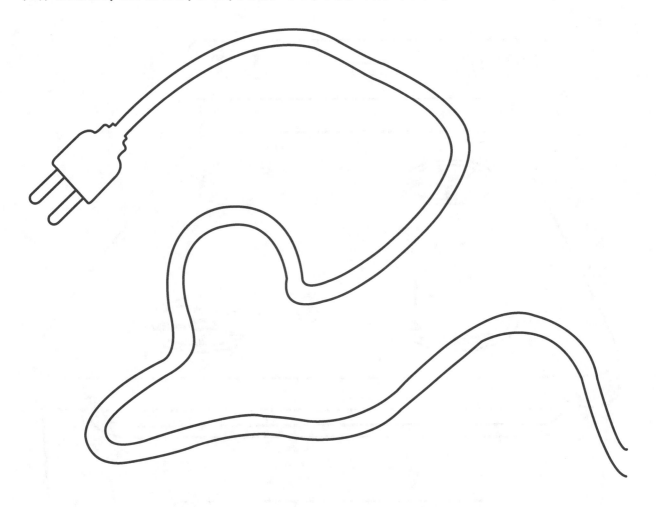

A5. HOT STOVE

A6. CABINET DOOR OPEN SHOWING CLEANING ITEMS

A7. HOT WATER IN BATHTUB

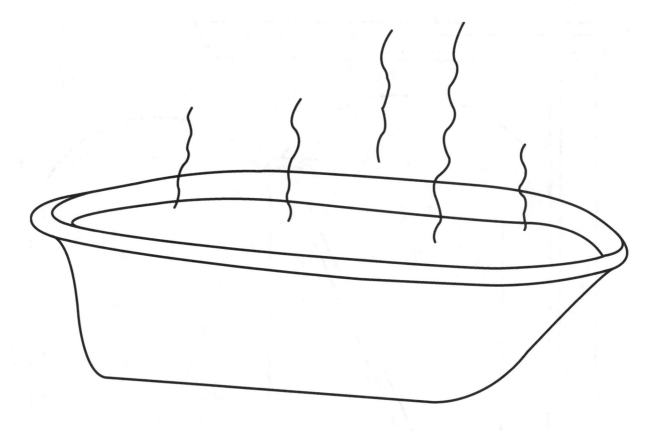

A8. FACE

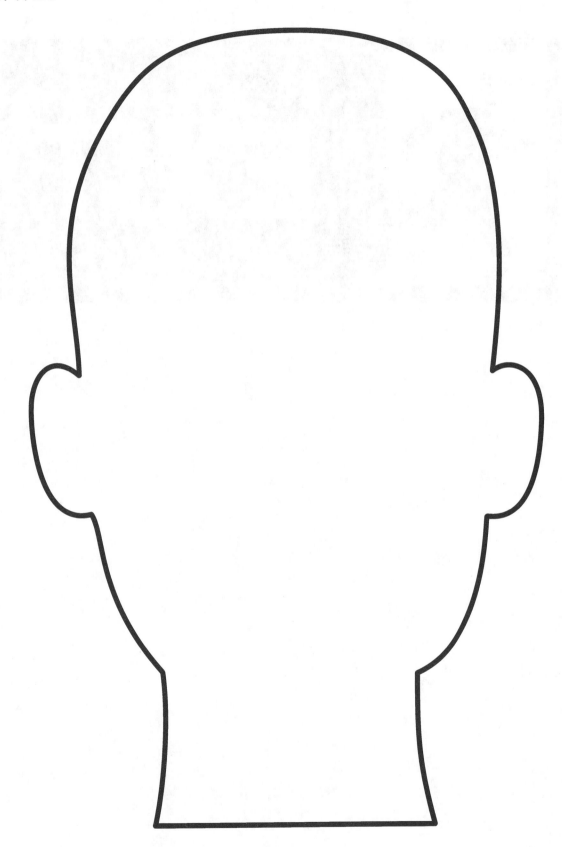

A9. EXIT SIGN

A10. TOOTH

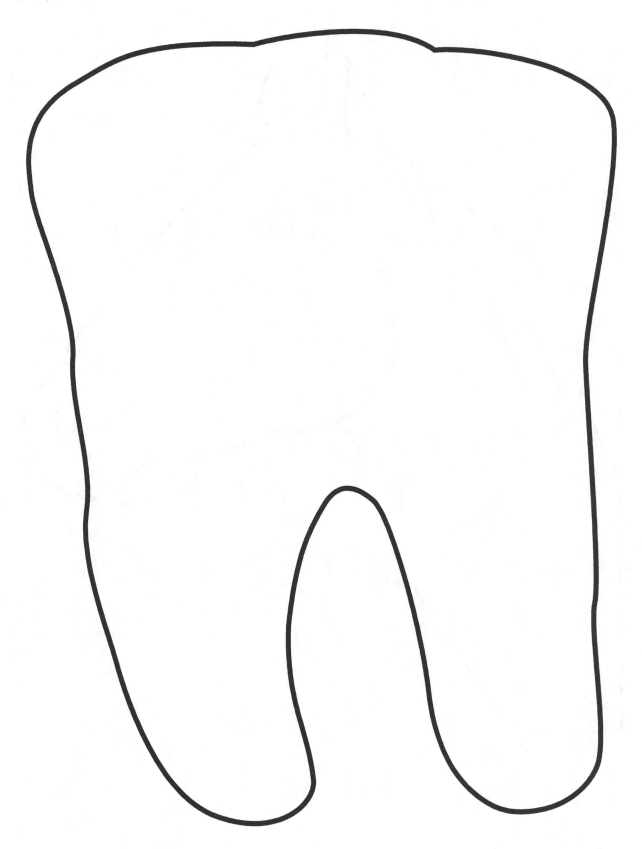

AII. HORSE HEAD

A13. PRESCRIPTION

Peter Piper, M. D
DEA# PP 2345765

2222 Pickled Pepper Lane, Suite #777   (770)555-3333
Mother Goose Land, GA 30848

NAME _____   AGE _____

ADDRESS _____

_____

DATE _____

RX

Refill_times

☐ Label

(Signature)

PEANUT BUTTER

A16. FISH

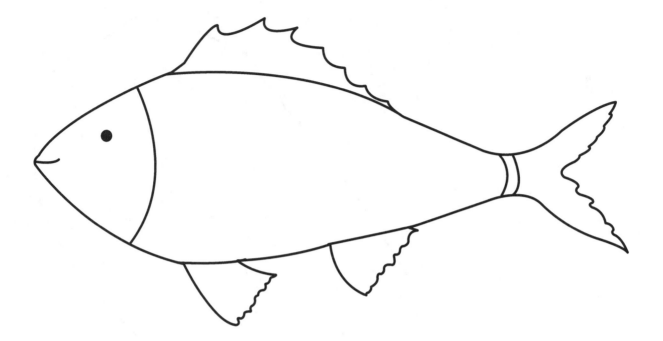

A17. CHICKEN DRUMSTICK

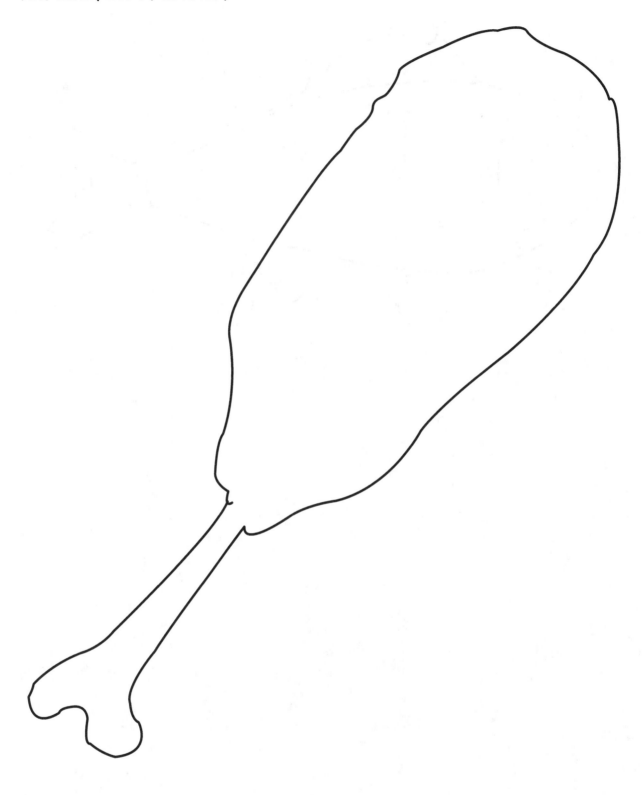

A18. PORK CHOP

A19. BEEF

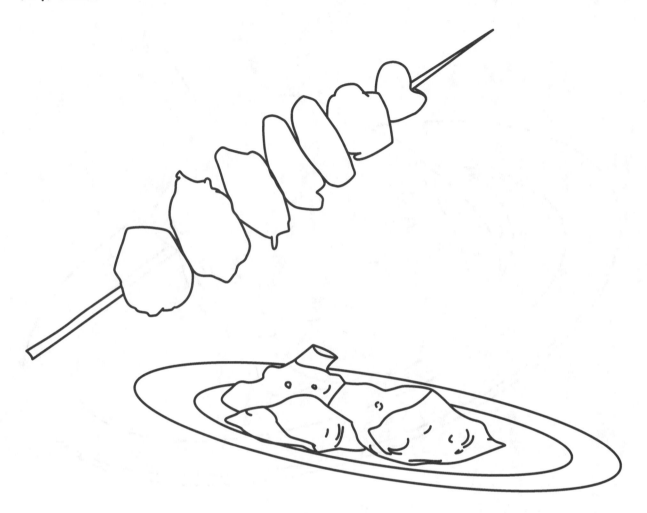

A20. EGG

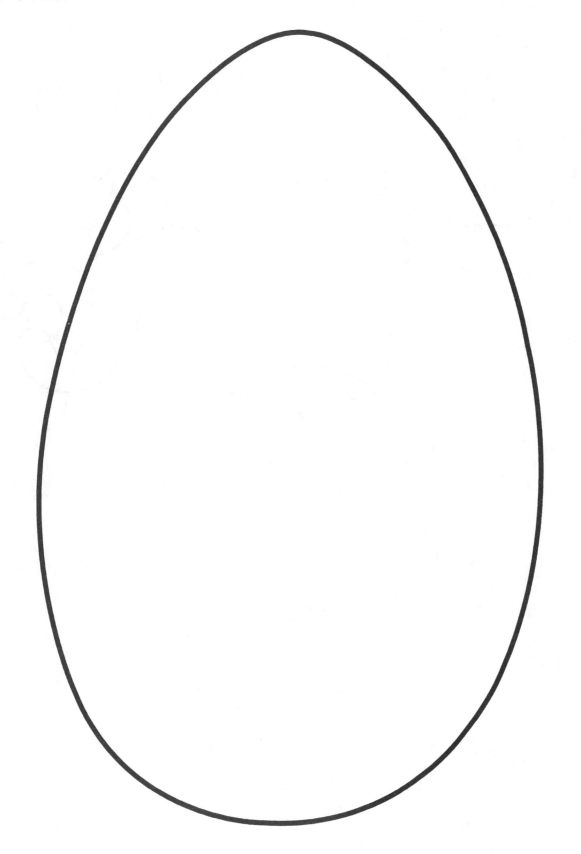

A21. NUTS

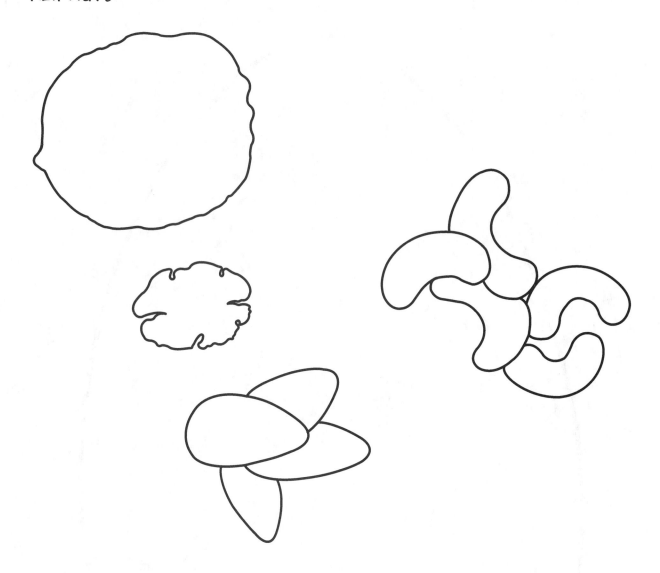

A22. HEART

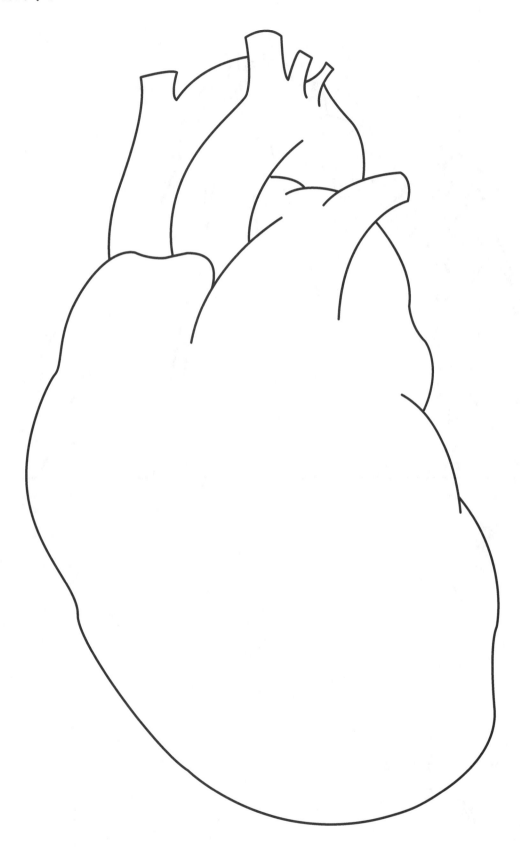

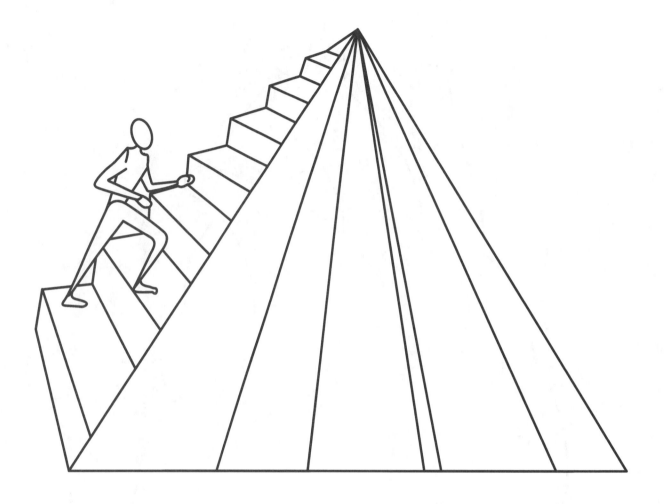

A24. STOP SIGN

A26. BIKE TRAIL

A27. WALK SIGNAL

A28. DON'T WALK SIGNAL

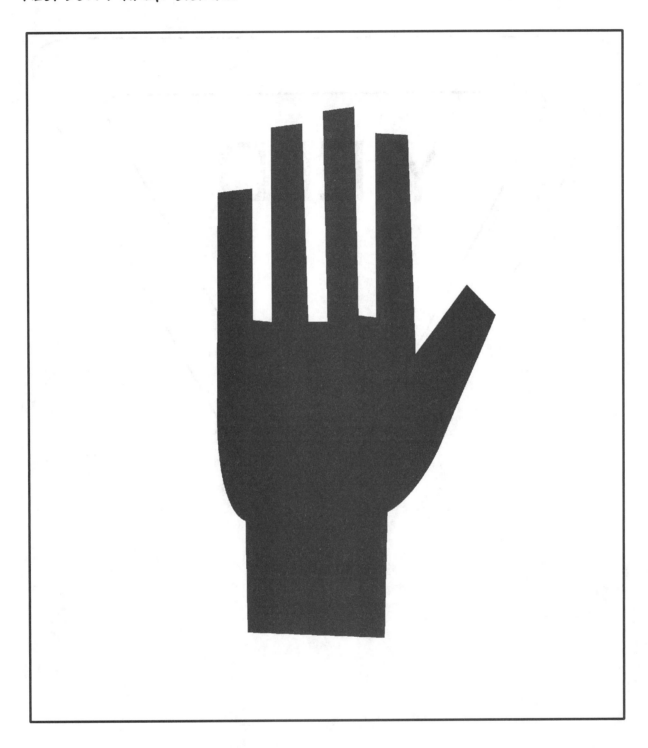

A29. YIELD SIGN

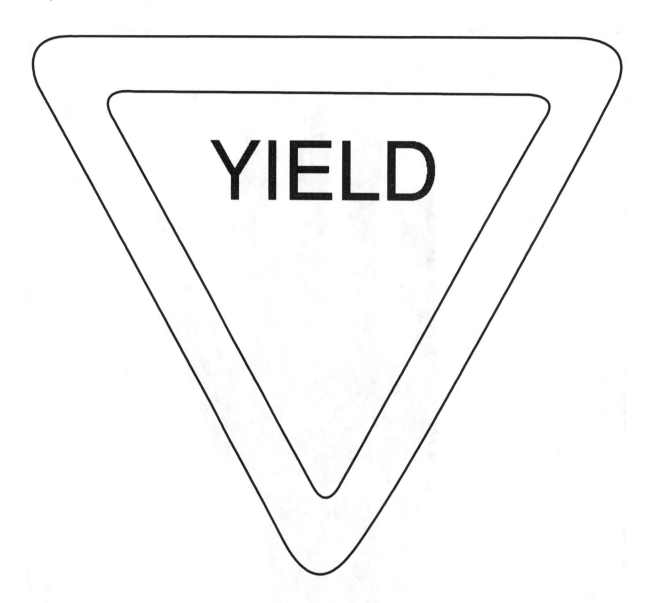

A30. TONGUE

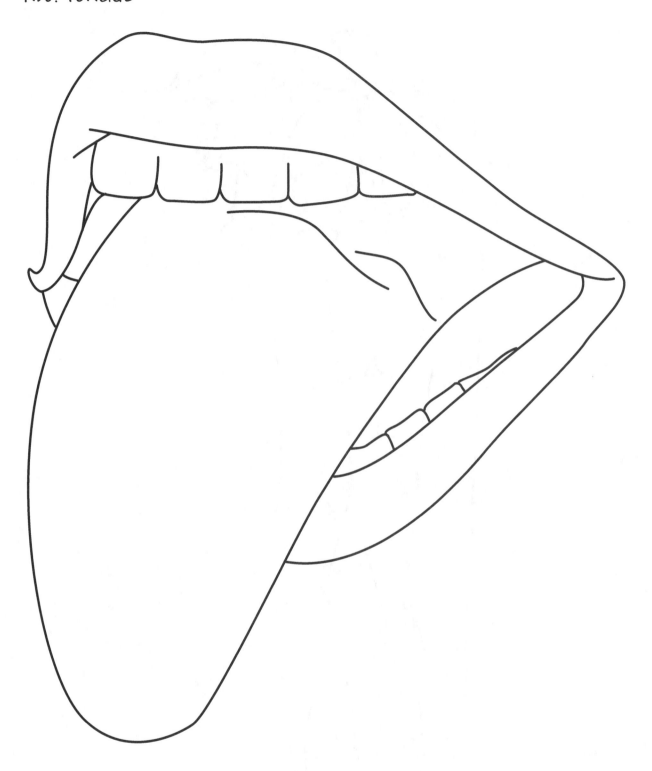

A31. CARROTS

A32. POTATO

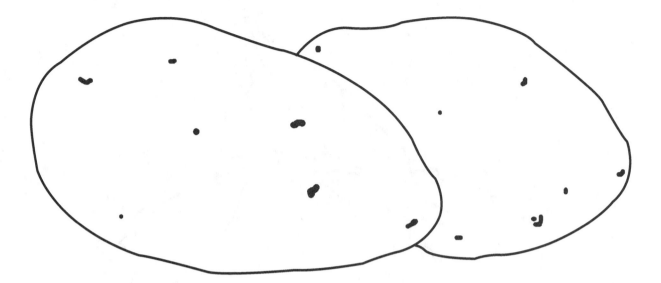

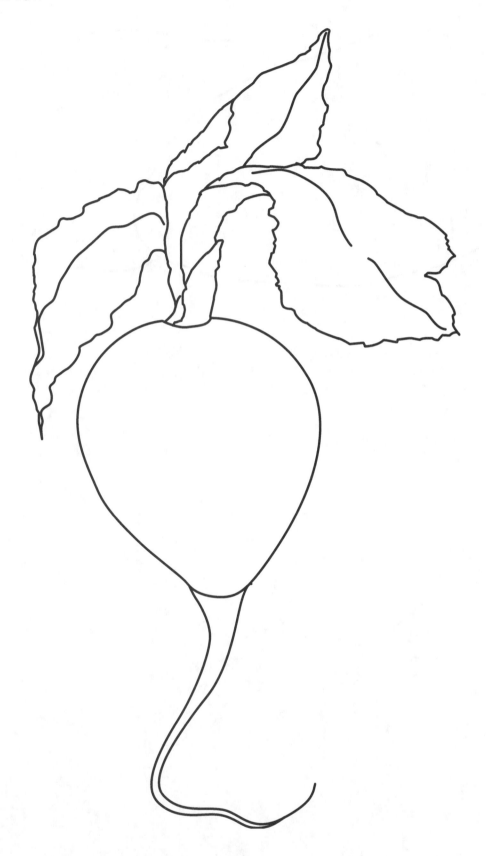

A34. YAMS

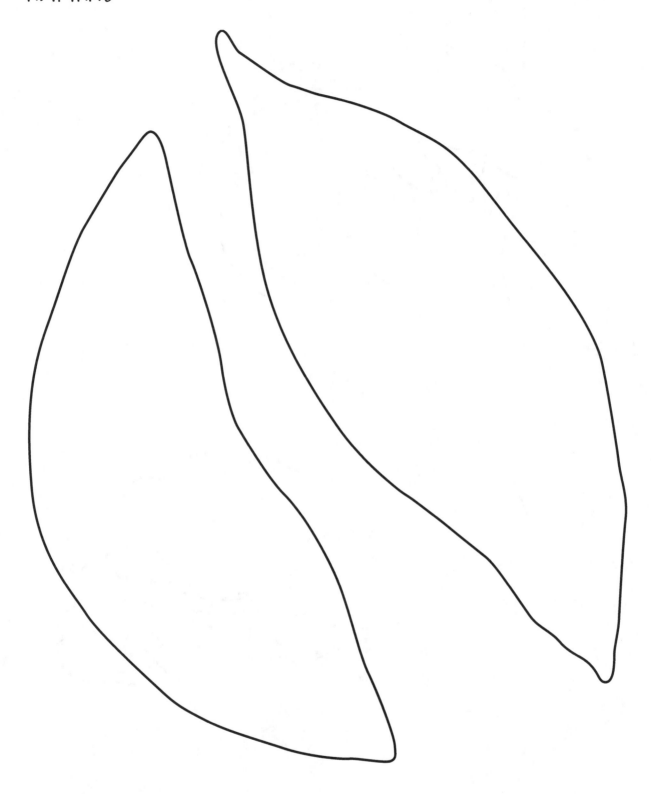

A35. BROCCOLI

A36. CORN

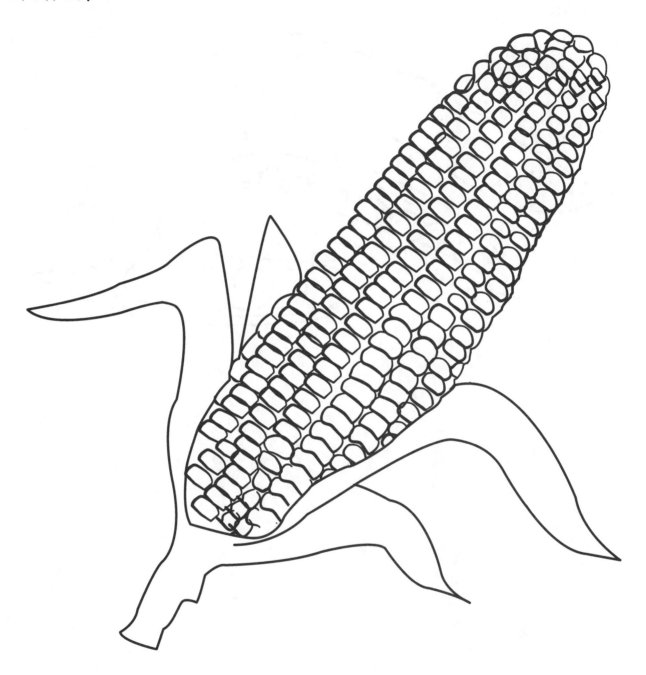

A37. PEAS

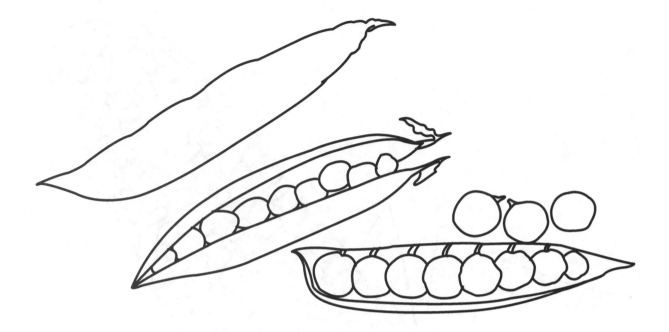

A38. PUMPKIN

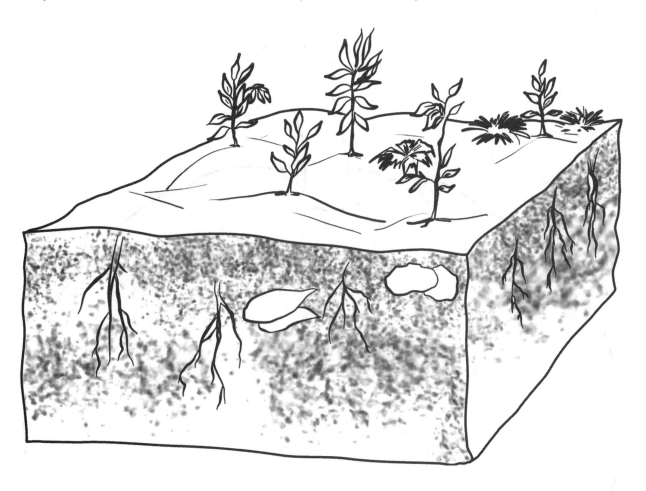

Appendix B

B1: Family Letter 1

Date:

Dear Family:

Our class will be making a class cookbook. Would you please fill in the attached form with one of your child's favorite nutritious recipes? Please return it by _____.

Thank you,

B2: Recipe form

_____'s favorite recipe for:

_____

Ingredients:

Instructions:

B3: Family Letter 2

Date:

Dear Family:

We are studying dental health in class. Dr. _____ donated the dental welcome bags. Attached is the tooth-brushing chart.

Please have your child use the items in the bag and help mark the dental chart.

Thank you,

B4: Tooth-brushing chart

	Sunday	Monday	Tuesday	Wednesday	Thursday	Friday	Saturday
Brush Teeth (sun)							
Brush Teeth (moon)							
Floss Teeth							

B5: Family Letter 3

Date:

Dear Family:

Enclosed is a chart for you and your child to fill in listing the items that your child had for dinner tonight. Please return the chart by _____.

We will make a class graph with the results.

Thank you,

B6: Food chart

Child's name:

Date:

Food Group	Type of food Examples	Type of food	Type of food
Grains	Rice		
Vegetables	Corn		
Fruits	Kiwi		
Milk and dairy products	Milk		
Meat, beans, fish, and nuts	Black beans		

B7: Permission form to be photographed and videotaped

My child, _____ has permission to be photographed or videotaped for educational purposes and/or class activities while attending _____.
(Child care center or school).

Parent's signature _____

Date _____

B8: Fingerprint card

Name					
Address					
Birth Date					
Parents or Guardian					
Phone numbers	Home Phone		Cell Phone		
	Work Phone		Pager		

Fingerprints

Right Thumb	Right Index	Right Middle	Right Ring	Right Little
Left Thumb	Left Index	Left Middle	Left Ring	Left Little

B9: Identification form

Place child's photo here	Name		
	Address		
	City	State	Zip code
	Phone		
	Birth date		

B10: Telephone card

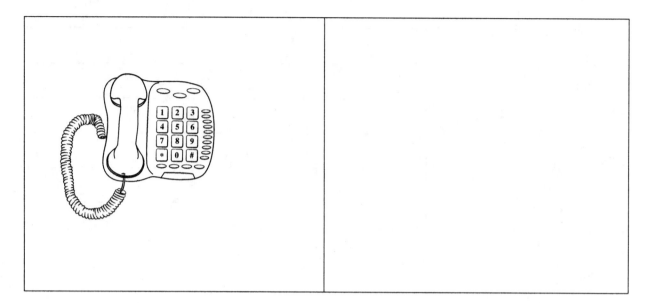

B11. Tea chart

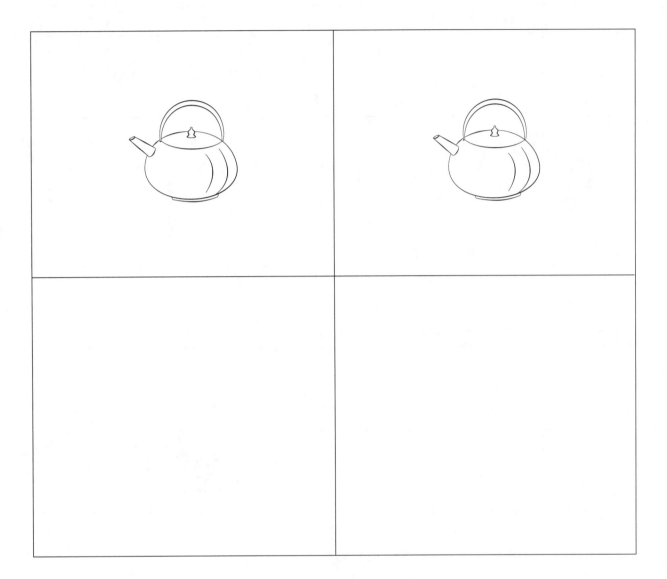

B12: Vitamin chart

Vitamins	What they help	
Vitamin A	Night vision and healthy skin	
Vitamin B	Digestion	
Vitamin C	Prevents infection	
Vitamin D	Bones and teeth	
Vitamin E	Antioxidant	
Vitamin K	Blood clotting	

Health Activities Index

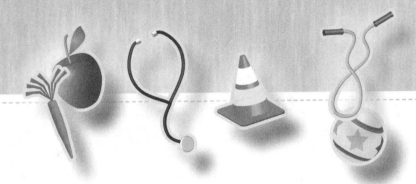

Safety Activities Index

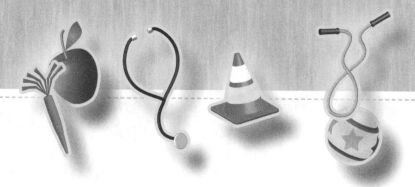

Nutrition Activities Index

Curriculum Index

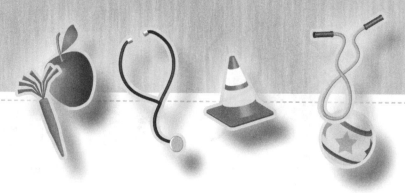

Index